First Person, Singular

First Person, Singular

Compiled by Jerry Jones
With Holly Miller

impact books

Nashville, TN

The author and publisher express appreciation to the following photographers for the use of their photographs:

Ann Kiemel/*Jack Gill*
Tim Sheppard/*Slick Lawson*
Joni Eareckson/*Jan Janura*
Harold Smith/*Russ Hanson*

First Person, Singular
© Copyright 1981 by IMPACT BOOKS, a division of The Benson Company, Inc. All rights reserved. Printed in the United States of America. No part of this book may be used or reproduced in any manner whatsoever without written permission, except in the case of brief quotations embodied in critical articles and reviews. For information: IMPACT BOOKS, a division of The Benson Company, Inc., 365 Great Circle Road, Nashville, Tennessee 37228.

First Printing September 1981

Distributed by The Zondervan Corporation

Library of Congress Cataloging in Publication Data
    Main Entry under title:
    First person, singular.
        1. Single people—Case studies. 2. Single people—Religious life—Case studies. I. Jones, Jerry, 1951– . II. Miller, Holly.
HQ800.F54   305   81-7131
ISBN 0-914850-81-4   AACR2
14018p

Scripture quotations are from the following sources:

HOLY BIBLE, *New International Version,* copyright © 1978, New York Bible Society. Used by permission.

Verses marked LB are taken from *The Living Bible,* copyright 1971 by Tyndale House Publishers, Wheaton, IL. Used by permission.

Contents

Preface

I've been sitting here looking out my cabin window. Everywhere I look I see a forest of green . . . tall majestic pine, fir, and cedar trees and a beautiful blanket of foliage. As the sun sets, the rich shades of green are becoming black.

It's not a dream, I remind myself. It's that long-awaited vacation to restore body, mind, and soul. I'm at Island Lake, a forty-minute ferry ride across the sound from Seattle, Washington—the perfect spot for writers, dreamers, or anyone else in need of some quiet and rest.

But before I get too laid back, there's a quick bit of work to be done. This preface must be written and sent to the publisher before they shut the book on me.

Earlier today I read through the final manuscript of *First Person, Singular*—a compilation of thoughts, ideas, opinions, and words of wisdom from twelve people. Each of them has something very worthwhile and beneficial to say to the single adult who desires a full life in Jesus

Christ. (Marrieds could benefit from reading this book as well.)

Some of the twelve are single and always have been. Some are single by death or divorce. And some are married. (And always have been, or so it seems!)

Although each of these people is quite well-known in Christian circles today, they are not to be looked upon as so-called Beautiful People set apart from the rest of us.

They are people made ordinary by the fact that they too have experienced loneliness, broken relationships, rejections, heartaches ... those situations in life without easy answers. But like you and me, they long to be loved uniquely, to be whole, and to know God as we were designed to know Him.

This book is not to take the place of searching God's Word for His answers and wisdom for your life. But it is an opportunity to benefit from what God has shown others in their adventure with Him.

And if the reader gains practical insight for his life through these people ... or simply realizes that he is not alone (other people hurt where he hurts, and overcome where he longs to overcome) ... then it will be worth the time and effort expended on this project.

One final note: I hope the reader will notice through these chapters the steady admonition to stay in God's Word as a part of a life style. There is nothing that can take the place of standing on the solid rock to get through the ups and downs of life.

So, enjoy!

Now, back to my vacation ...

Acknowledgments

The material in this book could not have been compiled without the help of several good people (and friends of *Solo*) across the country. Specifically they include: Linda Kay, Twila Knaack, Patty Pressler, Diane Procter, Harold Ivan Smith, and Beverly Wells.

These people made valuable contributions during the original *Solo* interviews. A special thanks to each one of them.

Also, a special thanks to Ed and Gwen Weising of Seattle and Barbara Calvo and all of the staff at Island Lake for providing one of my most refreshing vacations ever.

Ann Kiemel

*B*est-selling author and lecturer Ann Kiemel is a graduate of Northwest Nazarene College, and has done graduate work at Kansas University, Lawrence. She formerly served as a teacher, a church youth director, and the youngest dean of women in America. In addition to her full-time lecture ministry, she is the author of seven best-selling books and conducts an active tape ministry. Since Christmas, 1979, when she took twelve children and twelve adults to Israel to cheer her in a twenty-six-mile run around the Sea of Galilee, she has been involved in marathon running, and has participated in the Boston Marathon.

Publisher's Note:

Since the publication of this article in Solo *magazine, Ann Kiemel was married in Boston in June, 1981.*

13

Ann Kiemel

One on One

Thump.

The juice on her tray barely quivered in its clear plastic cone as the jet touched down. She shook the drowsiness from her head. On a scale of one to ten, as her teen-age neighbor liked to say, the flight had been an eleven. Smooth takeoff, friendly attendants, hot lunch, an extra-interesting seatmate, and (bonus!) an on-time arrival.

But the day was just beginning . . . there was still lots of time left for snags. Somewhere in the mass of smiling, waving plane-greeters was a lovely Christian couple—just names to her now—whose mission was to retrieve her from the stream of travelers spilling out of the plane's cabin ("Look for a gray plaid suit," she had advised) and deliver her to a nearby Holiday Inn. *Would they be there? Would they recognize her? What if the luggage went on to Louisville like it did last week? Ugh.*

"Welcome to Des Moines." She read the message

curled around the airport tower as the plane taxied smoothly to the accordian-like gate. *Des Moines?* She nervously searched her purse for a crumpled itinerary. Relief. *Des Moines on Tuesday, Milwaukee tomorrow, a stopover in Chicago, then home to Boston for the weekend.*

The afternoon schedule looked cramped. She had less than two hours to unpack, blot some powder on her freckled nose, steam the wrinkles from her good dress (providing it was in Des Moines, too), and collect her thoughts for the evening's speech. Also shoehorned between now and the end of the day would be dinner with members of the sponsoring church, a drive to a crowded hall, an hour onstage, an autograph session afterward, and finally, her daily run—ten miles of it.

"You're so lucky," said a wistful voice.

Ann Kiemel looked up into a pretty but tired face. Smiles were traded and a book thrust forward for an autograph.

"Your life is so exciting," continued the woman. "The travel, speeches, writing books, touching lives, talking about Jesus. Sometimes I think the only thing I'm good for is fixing three meals a day, ironing my husband's shirts, and driving carpools."

"What's your name?" asked Ann.

"Judy."

To Judy, she scrawled across the leaflet. *Remember, Jesus is counting on you to be His woman in Des Moines. He loves you and I do too. Ann.*

There were many things she might have said to Judy of Des Moines and to all the other Judys she meets on the road each year. They come in droves, lured by her simple books with the big messages; her taped testimony, delivered in squeaky little-girl tones; her talk show appearances with the few well-chosen words which say so much. They look at her with envy, glamorizing her single-ness, freedom, and no-strings status—a modern-day crusader who unabashedly admits she's out to change the world.

Fans feel the tug of toddlers on their jeans and the pull of a budget's stretching to cover the needs of two, three, or four people. Being creative, growing in spirit-uality, and becoming a positive force in other people's lives seem so appealing. If only each day didn't include an endless list of *must do's!* (We must do laundry, drive swim team carpool, attend PTA meetings, decorate cookies for the Scout bake sale. . .)

Yet part of Ann's message urges Christians to accept their places in life creatively. Too often, she believes, Christians waste time and energy which could be used for Jesus, saying, "If only . . . "

"Obedience should mean no compromises, yet we make so many. I think single people make as many, or more, compromises than anybody, especially in the area of sex, and in their mental outlook.

"I believe it's a sin to be unhappy in the will of God—to compare ourselves to others, always thinking that somebody else's life is better than ours, saying, 'If only I had *her* husband or *his* wife; if only I lived in *their* house, or had *that* job, or looked like *she* does,'" she stresses. "I am who I am; God rules my being, and I am to let Him be creative with who I am. Until we learn to be happy with God's will for us, He cannot be creative in us."

Ann Kiemel practices what she preaches. Being un-attached in a society dominated by married couples was never her goal or expectation. Growing up in Hawaii, the daughter of missionary parents, she often played "house" with twin sister Jan. They invented whole families to hover over, and many times spent long, humid after-noons under the backyard trees, enjoying picnics with their imaginary children. Half of these dreams came true—today Jan is happily married and lives in Ohio with her husband and two beautiful children. "House" hasn't materialized for Ann—at least, not yet.

"Holidays are the hardest for me," she says. "For instance, when I go home for Christmas, and it's time to go to bed, my sister and her husband go in one room, my brother and his wife go into another, my parents go off to their room. Then I am left to decide where I'm going to sleep."

Ann Kiemel, lonely? Fans would say that's incredible. But she's human, after all, and loneliness is a state of being which all people face—occasionally, if not daily. Even persons like Ann who lead busy, rich lives still succumb to one-sided, soul-searching, inquisitions: *Is this all there is? Doesn't anyone care? Am I really needed? What's my pupose, anyway?*

"Sometimes it's not so much loneliness as it is just standing alone in the world," she explains. "It's being on your own, being responsible for your own happiness, fun, and creative outlets. Everything is up to you. I don't always like that responsibility. I would love to have someone come grab me up to take care of me."

But she's learning. And she's coping.

"Ten years ago I was a different single woman from the one I am today. It has taken lots of years, months, and days to get to the place where I am now. It is a process. You can't go from *A* to *B* overnight. I'm really at a very good place in my life right now. God has led me here and I'm very content. Yet, although I'm not engulfed in loneliness, I still have to deal with it."

Like many single women, Ann says her loneliness goes deeper than outward appearances might indicate. Her successes as a writer and speaker keep her in demand. She's with people constantly in her public life and is surrounded by a large circle of friends in private moments. She remains close to her neighbors and spends hours each week visiting with female friends, baking cookies with the kids down the block, and enjoying lunch with couples in her apartment building. But the tough part, she admits, is coming home after a long day, wanting to be nurtured, needing to be held, and longing to be close to someone.

She believes obedience to God's will is her key to coping with physical and mental loneliness. Such obedience once didn't seem important but, today, it is the secret to her fulfillment. It has led her beyond mere acceptance of her singleness to welcoming the challenge.

"Singles often compromise their potential. They say, 'I can't do as much, be as creative, or be quite as happy and productive. I don't have the opportunities.'"

Sound like a compromise? Ann thinks so. She urges singles to explore the possibilities and the advantages.

"Being a single woman allows me the freedom to invite children in and have them stay overnight. I can have couples over for dinner. I'm challenged by all the opportunities Jesus gives me in my own neighborhood. For too many singles, it's just easier to compromise and do less than the best."

She's progressed to the point where she no longer thinks of herself as a "single," but as a woman and as a person. While she had always envisioned herself going through life as a helpmate to a husband, she accepts the idea that God may have other plans for her. These plans are no better, or no worse, than those He has for Judy of Des Moines. Just different.

She was once asked if she thought being a single adult is contrary to God's basic plan and design for His people. Her answer? An emphatic no!

"God's master plan can involve more of our lives if we will just give Him time and room to develop it. A lot of times the reason we are single or the reason we are limited in our singleness is that we are wishing God would move us somewhere else. We haven't learned to be creative and committed where we are now."

Yet she hopes to marry someday. This hope comes not because she feels incomplete in her "oneness" but because she thinks no other relationship in the world provides the test and commitment of marriage—a situation in which somebody will know her better than anybody else, live with her twenty-four hours a day, be her true and honest critic, and blend his life with hers while she's learning to blend hers with his.

"I don't think my being married would enhance my basic relationship with Jesus Christ in terms of my ministry. Neither do I need a man to establish my identity or to feel right about my place in the world. I feel very okay where I am—being single. Being married wouldn't make me 'better.'

"I would only marry because I really loved the man and because we both felt it was God's will. I want to learn to give and share in a tested kind of relationship where I'm not the heroine but half of a partnership. I want to learn to mesh my loves, my desires, my wishes, and my needs with those of somebody else. As I see it, to have a successful marriage, one has to be unselfish and surrendered."

She blames the current high rate of divorce on the lack of commitment by many marriage partners. The fact that her parents have remained happily married for forty years reinforces her belief in the commitment. The senior Kiemels work at their relationship to keep it healthy and intact.

"I can't say that my mother and father have had a passionate kind of love affair all their lives, but I know that they have had a good life together. I know it's as much a credit to my mother as to my father. They have both shared and given. They have really been a team. When my father, a minister for many years, would come in and say, 'Well, we're moving,' I can never remember once hearing my mother complain. If my father was going, she was committed to him. Their relationship has paid off by nurturing some strong points in their children. We might not have developed those points had my mother been an overly dominant woman who pushed my dad around, or who degraded him by saying or acting like he had silly ideas or wasn't strong or wasn't the leader. We girls have developed a great sense of security because we knew our parents had a solid relationship."

Any commitment she might make to a man will be similar to the kind her mother made to her dad. It won't be built on a high-pitched emotionalism or sensuality or excitement. It will be based on her belief that he is God's man for her and they can make more out of life together than apart.

But should she never marry, her answer to Jesus is still yes. She realizes that there are some people who are meant to remain single and are more significant in the world because of it. When she served as youth director at a large church in California, she was grateful for her singleness. She spent long hours with families—parents, as well as teen-agers. She could never have given those hours had she been married.

"Today a marriage commitment would mean certain changes in my life style. However, I don't believe a woman loses her identity when she merges her life with that of a marriage partner. I don't think God would say to me, 'Ann, I made you to be a creative person with certain gifts and certain strengths until you become thirty-four. Now I'm going to have you marry and strip you of all that.' Certainly I would have to give up some things, but I could cope with that. I'm not building my life and my security around being an author and speaker. I'm trying very hard to build my life around the things that are real. It mustn't matter how much money I have, or what kind of clothes are in my closet, or who reads my books. I have to ask, *Jesus, are You the center of me?* Anything else seems superficial."

Her schedule—her whole life style—does not lend itself to meeting Christian men. None of her male friends in her historic Boston neighborhood is Christian, and on the road she is whisked from one obligation to the next without time to develop more than passing friendships. She's so committed to her ministry that she doesn't think about her single status and how it might be altered. When she stands in front of an audience, she is not wondering if her husband-to-be might be looking back at her. When she's autographing books and notices a nice-looking man in the line she doesn't think, *Hmmm, I wonder if he's single?* She decided a long time ago that if God has a special man for her, He'll put their lives together. She knows the man He chooses for her will appreciate her for herself, not for her ministry or public image.

Many men approach her, awed by her following and intrigued by her message. They question, *Is she real?* Even after careful scrutiny, some still don't fully understand her commitment and her priorities. She never compromises the belief that Jesus must always come first.

"Hardly a day goes by without some kind of social contact with an attractive, challenging man. But I think the answer is learning not to give double messages; being able to go out to dinner with a man, and being able to walk away afterward.

"I've reached that point now, but I haven't always been there. Sometimes, in the past, I have not been at that pure committed place of wanting to obey Jesus more than I wanted to fill an emotional need. In the past I have responded to men out of a need for security or a need to feel appealing, or from a need to be loved by a man. Those are double messages and unfair to the man. I'm learning to say no a lot."

But saying no sometimes results in losing a special friend. Often a man wants more from a relationship than she is willing to give without compromise.

She's found that sometimes such misunderstandings can be avoided if early in a relationship the single woman sets the framework for the budding friendship. Often this requires a flat statement—"I don't want to get involved; let's be friends"—that is difficult to make. Ann remembers times of insecurity when she failed to make the statement and her intentions were misinterpreted. Now she not only makes the statement verbally but communicates it through her actions, dress, and even her mannerisms. Her total message is that she is a happy, well-adjusted single woman who is not actively seeking a mate, but whose energies are directed toward God's work in her world.

This message, strengthened and polished through experience, was fostered by her parents years ago. Just as her mother prepared Jan and Ann for the traditional roles of wife and mother, the Kiemels also taught their children a more valuable lesson—how to be responsible, caring Christians, whether married or single. Yes, they were shown how to cook, sew, and balance the household accounts, but they were also put through less common paces. About once a week Mrs. Kiemel sat each of the kids in a different room with the order: "I want you to think for thirty minutes." How they hated it! They didn't want to *think,* they wanted to play. But their mother explained, "People don't think enough today; people don't think about where they're going, what they want to do with their lives, what their dreams are."

The Kiemels also taught the children to give their best. Ann decided years ago if she were really to make a difference in her neighborhood she must work much longer and much harder than the traditional eight hours a day. Her nonstop schedule has caused some Annwatchers to dub her a workaholic. She replies that she can't make a mark in the world if she's less-than-wholehearted in her work. Others dismiss her as a Pollyanna.

"There are many days when I don't feel great. But I don't live my life by my feelings. When I'm frustrated, my first human tendency is to become engulfed in my mood. My second response is to shake it off. Why make it such a big problem? Life is not heavy. I'm not racked with pain, lying in a bed. I'm not wondering where my next meal is coming from. God has been so good to me. Why should I let my feelings cover up all His goodness?"

Of course it's not easy. She works at dispelling negative feelings by verbalizing them. If she feels depressed, she says so. Five minutes later she might be laughing and working through it. She never allows herself to go to bed feeling down—that's too much like crawling away from the world. She keeps moving. Why? She believes a person chooses to be happy or unhappy. Each individual chooses to see the good or the bad in people, including himself. If everyone would only surrender to God, life would be beautiful.

"Joni Eareckson is one of the greatest examples. When I sit and talk to her, she is so beautiful and so genuine and has such a sparkle in her eyes that I'm not even aware of her crippled state. She had the choice of living by her feelings, just as we all have the option of being happy or unhappy."

She knows everyone isn't a Joni Eareckson or an Ann Kiemel, but she believes everyone can be just as dedicated to a purpose or mission. From many of the letters she receives from her peers, the message is, "Ann, I can't do what you do or live where you live, but I can love in my own world. Until I read your books, I never thought about all the people around me. I never thought about my neighborhood. I never thought about my job. I used to think, *I just work at a desk, so what can I do?* Now I know I can love in my own world. You've given me new ideas as to how I can love creatively in my own world."

Correspondence streams in from people who work in offices. They tell of efforts to reach out and touch the lives of co-workers. "I started by taking someone to lunch," related one correspondent. "Then I began to see everyone in a way I'd never seen them before. I saw people who need to be loved . . . people with hurts and struggles . . . people who need Jesus Christ."

To be an effective witness for Jesus, Ann believes a person can be married, single, young, old, a resident of Boston (like she is) or of Des Moines (like Judy), or any other neighborhood in the world. Most important, he or she must be committed to Christ, willing to obey His will, and dedicated to living a disciplined life. It takes discipline to pull everything together. Ann, for instance, keeps a pad and pen by her bed, and if she wakes up during the night, she writes down things that need to be done the next day. It's a top priority for her to be organized and disciplined. It takes hard work; it takes getting up early and going long days. She admits a person must work harder if he or she wants to accomplish a lot of extra objectives.

Running every day has helped her to become more disciplined. She gets up at 5:30 A.M. to jog and usually doesn't get to bed until midnight. It takes a lot of commitment to squeeze running into an already full schedule, but she likes it, looks good because of it, and believes the exercise contributes to her vibrant good health. Her original motivation—*Jesus, who could I meet while running?* —has enabled her to meet some unusual Bostonians.

Discipline also involves spiritual as well as physical exercise. She reads the Word every day no matter how she feels, and tries to read the Bible through each year, in various translations.

"I never sit down to read without a pen in my hand. I know if I read with a pen in hand, expecting to mark something, I'm more in tune and am ready to pick up on any little thing that might touch my life in some way. I read three chapters a day, two from the Old Testament and one from the New. I've grown to really love God's Word, but there are days when it takes real discipline to sit down and read. It also takes real discipline to put on my running shoes and exercise. But, I know if I'm going to be the best person I can be, I have to be a balanced person. If I tour all over the country and talk about God's love and I'm not a real Christian in my own neighborhood, I have nothing to say to the world. If I write twenty books and am not really careful about my own physical, mental, and spiritual health, then I can't do my best for God."

She must also remain flexible and willing to accept any new project or assignment God has for her. When she was a child she never dreamed of being an author and a speaker. In earlier years she had confessed, *Jesus, I don't know where I'm going. I don't know what You're going to do with me.*

She never viewed herself as an extremely creative person, but she offered whatever talents she had to Him with the words: *I am Yours and You are great. If we get together and I really follow You, what are the creative ways You can use me in the world?*

She never would have guessed His plans for her.

"My real ambition, all my life, has been to be God's woman, to be a true Christian. That was my ambition fifteen years ago, and it is still my ambition today. I don't care about writing ten more books and being a well-known author, or addressing 200,000 more people in the next twelve months. My ambition is to be true to Him. My dreams are built around all the creative ways I can touch the world with God's love."

Neither does she worry about the future.

"I don't think this is where I'm going to be forever. Everybody's not going to want to hear me speak, and I don't know how many more books I'm going to write. All I know about is today. Jesus is the Lord of my life today—and I give Him this day my very best. To every person I encounter—from the cab driver to the waitress—I want to give my best. And when the day is over, I'll start tomorrow.

"I'm doing what I am today because Jesus led me here . . . it's God's will for my life today. His great love has given me this time to fail, struggle, fight, evolve, resolve, and to work through many issues in my life. When it's time for Him to lead me on to some new place—whether it's slowing down and marrying or writing another book—He will let me know."

If she has succeeded in touching people's lives—especially other singles—it is because she understands them. She struggles with all the human temptations, all the human feelings, all the fears anyone else has. She suffers bouts of loneliness and deals with self-doubts daily. She knows there are many single people in the world who feel like misfits . . . inadequate and incomplete.

"I'd be less than honest if I were to throw them pat statements like, 'You are beautiful,' 'You are great,' 'You are somebody.' I'm sorry for their pain and I understand it. I grew up feeling very insecure. As a youngster in Hawaii, I was surrounded by beautiful children so very different from myself. I was fair and tall and blue-eyed; they were dark and petite and brown-eyed. So I have felt and experienced those human pains and I know it's not easy feeling different, no matter what the reason."

She urges singles to work at being happy and at accepting the fact that Jesus is in them and that He has put them where they are for a purpose. She believes He can transform lives into creative and exciting forces in the world.

"If I build around who Ann is, that's ego. But if I build around who God is, His creativity can expand my life in ways I would never dream possible.

"I'm happy today. I'm happy being single because it is God's will for me right now. It's not always easy, but being married wouldn't always be easy either. I'm happy being Ann Kiemel. I don't always like Ann Kiemel. I don't always like dealing with her insecurities. I don't always like how she looks. I don't always like how she plays tennis. I don't always like how she writes. But I like being Ann Kiemel because Jesus made Ann Kiemel. Jesus lives in me, and He wants to do something in me and through me."

And she underscores that statement of faith with the two words that have become her manifesto, *Yes, Lord!*

"I believe it's a sin to be unhappy in the will of God—to compare ourselves to others, always thinking that somebody else's life is better than ours, saying 'If only I had her husband or his wife; if only I lived in their house, or had that job, or looked like she does,' I am who I am; God rules my being, and I am to let Him be creative with who I am. Until we learn to be happy with God's will for us, He cannot be creative in us."

Tom Netherton

*A*ll-American Tom Netherton is actually a native of Munich, Germany, the son of a career Army officer. He attended the University of Minnesota, leaving in 1966 to join the Army, where he received the Army, Navy, and Air Force Spirit of Honor Medal and the Army Commendation Medal. He also attended the Bethany Fellowship Missionary Training Center in Minnesota for a year and a half.

In response to a strong pull in the direction of the entertainment field, his singing career reached its peak in 1973 with his first appearance on the "Lawrence Welk Show." Between engagements, he appears in supper clubs, theaters, churches, musicals, and hotels. He has recorded six record albums.

Tom Netherton

New Directions

Baton in hand, Lawrence Welk stood motionless in front of his famous bandstand, waiting for the cue indicating the end of another sixty-second salespitch. Five. Four. Three. Two. One . . .

"Ladies and gentlemen, here's our young *single* boy, Tom Netherton, to sing you a song. Ready, Tom? One-and-a-two-and . . ."

He had done it again—in his introduction, Mr. Welk had accentuated Tom's *single* status. Tom acknowledged the applause, knowing he could expect a fresh deluge of letters from eligible young girls, mothers of eligible young girls, and grandmothers of eligible young girls. And those eligible young girls would be more than willing to board the next flight West to arrange a let's-get-acquainted date. Some proposals aren't as predictable, though, and every batch of mail contains at least a few surprises.

"I once got a note from a lady which said, 'I heard

you're single and are looking for a wife. If no one else will marry you, I will.' To show she meant business, she included a picture of herself in a bathing suit. She was eighty-six years old and I think her swimsuit was too. Depression era, anyway. I couldn't believe it," he laughs.

If there's any such thing as "the girl next door," Tom is her male counterpart. What mother wouldn't love to introduce him to her Wednesday bridge club with the words: "You know my son-in-law, Tom Netherton? The one who sings on the 'Lawrence Welk Show'?" Blond, perfectly groomed, former senior class president, decorated serviceman, Tom is the answer to every matchmaker's dream. He lacks only the Good Housekeeping Seal of Approval.

"But what you see on TV is not always what you get," cautions Tom. "I realize people sometimes say things about me out of ignorance. They don't know the real me. When I get letters from grandmothers suggesting that they have a granddaughter who would be perfect for me, I wonder, honestly, how anybody can say that when the only 'me' they know is the one they see on TV. The public me. The façade. For all they know, I could turn out to be a wife-beater! It saddens me that so many people make quick, superficial judgments. I have friends, family, and problems just like anyone else. We're all real people with real struggles."

And Tom's greatest struggle, like that of so many other show business personalities, seems to be loneliness. Road tours often stretch on for weeks—even months —while time at home in Los Angeles can be counted in days—even hours. He blames himself, not his life style, for his feeling of being alone, and he claims it has nothing to do with circumstances themselves, but his reactions to circumstances.

"I've been lonely a big part of my life. On the outside, I've always been ready for good times, laughter, and fun.

But on the inside, I seldom felt close to others. I used to want to be someone else. I disliked the way I looked—I was too tall; I wanted to be dark-complexioned and have dark hair. I always felt 'they' were over there, that 'they' all knew each other, were all friends, and here I was over here by myself. When I first moved to the Los Angeles area, I went through a really tough time. The public me would be out meeting lots of people, signing autographs, and shaking hands; then the private me had to come back home alone.

"I like my home and am comfortable in it, yet I have no one with whom to share it. If not some *one,* at least some *people.* In my case, I'm gone so much of the time that I don't have many chances to develop deep friendships. To many people I'm an ideal ... the all-American Christian young man. (That's why all those grandmothers try to introduce me to their granddaughters.) And I long for close relationships. Sometimes I wonder, *Does anyone really care about me personally?"*

He claims his feelings of insecurity date back to his Minnesota childhood when he spent hours and hours dreaming about growing up to become "somebody." While self-doubts were painful to Tom, the boy, he believes now they were necessary to the growth of Tom, the man. He determined to achieve as an adult all the things he felt he lacked as a child.

"I think some of the most successful people are those who basically feel insecure. There is a driving desire to prove they *are* someone. That has been a real struggle through my Christian years—to become aware that I am important simply because I belong to God. He made me, and my importance is not because of who I am or because of my talents, but because God created me and made me the object of His affection. That's the way it is for all of us."

Learning to deal with loneliness and insecurity has been a slow process for Tom. He's found that by turning his thoughts and concerns toward others rather than focusing them on himself, he can overcome his negative feelings.

"We must realize that many, many people in this world—our friends, neighbors, people with whom we go to church—are terribly lonely. They may not admit it because they think Christians aren't supposed to be lonely. Isn't the perfect Christian always supposed to have the joy of the Lord? Even many pastors struggle with this. Personally, I feel that I've got to reach out to heal the hurts and pain in other people's lives instead of concentrating on my own hurts and pain."

Difficult to do? Sure, sometimes. But Tom believes that by shifting his vision from himself to the Lord, he is able to see people as God might see them and he becomes sensitive to their needs. Whereas he once felt intimidated by persons who did not smile at him in just the right way or act positively toward him, now he looks beyond such superficial expressions.

"I just ask the Lord to let me see people through His eyes," he explains. "As I looked out at the audience during a recent concert, I started seeing individuals instead of a mass of people. I saw hurt and loneliness and crushed personalities and people longing to be loved. I just couldn't get away from it. I'd like to be able to apply God's love on an individual basis. I want to minister. I want something extra special to happen, something beyond the applause that is a part of any show. I don't want to be just a singer who gives a testimony, makes people laugh and cry, or causes them to comment on how well he can sing. I'd like them to go home saying, 'I want to know God better.' I want them to see their own value and to know Jesus loves them all the way."

The need for such a ministry is becoming more evident to Tom as he travels and becomes more sensitive to his audiences. And, although he's grateful to mass media for amplifying his talents and increasing his fame as a performer, he blames them for encouraging people to compare themselves with others. He cites magazine articles and TV shows that hype superstar images and devote too much time and space to the so-called Beautiful People. Readers and viewers tend to compare themselves with such personalities and walk away with self-doubts and insecurities. He believes that God wants us to develop our own unique potential. This knowledge has helped him accept himself—blond hair, fair complexion, and all—and even to love himself.

"Something happened to me when I was in the Army, stationed in Panama, that I think is applicable to all who need to learn self-acceptance," he recalls. "I saw a beautiful girl singing in the choir at the church I attended. Immediately I started wondering how I might meet her and, more importantly, how I could impress her. Then something clicked inside. I realized that if I started dating her she was going to find out soon enough what I was really like. Since she was bound to discover the *real* me, why should I try to be somebody else? Why not just be myself? If she liked me, fine. If not, that was the way it was supposed to be. This released me and helped me to relax and ask her for a date.

"We can't worry because we don't look like someone we admire, or because our hair isn't the color we think is desirable to other people. We have to learn to say, 'Hey, I'm me. I don't feel the need to impress someone.' Such an attitude can really free us to explore and enjoy a wide variety of new relationships."

Fame presents a different set of problems and insecurities. It can sometimes deter a special friendship, causing it to founder before it progresses beyond the casual stage. Tom admits he is often suspicious when a woman shows an obvious interest in him. And not without reason. On more than one occasion he's discovered an aspiring singer wants him to use his influence to get her an audition for the "Lawrence Welk Show."

"Many times I feel a woman wants to be with me because she wants to be seen with 'someone.' I want to be cared about and loved because I'm me, because the woman enjoys my company, not because I'm on television. Many times, I've been introduced as 'Tom Netherton from the "Lawrence Welk Show."' I'd like to just be introduced as Tom Netherton. Period."

It works both ways, though, and Tom admits succumbing to the temptation of name-dropping.

"It's something we all really have to watch. Basically, name-dropping means that, to be accepted in life, we have to be associated with someone else, assuming their popularity as our own. After I've been around much-better-known entertainers than I, I catch myself saying, 'I've just been to such-and-such party with so-and-so.' My motive was to make myself look more important. God does not want me to get my acceptance through someone else. He has made me who I am."

On a recent Hawaiian vacation, Tom was able to savor a welcome taste of anonymity. He became acquainted with a group of Australian tourists, totally unfamiliar with the Welk show. Entertainers themselves, they never mentioned their own fame to Tom.

"It was so refreshing to be treated as a normal person. I had to find out about their fame from others, and when they learned of mine, they weren't at all impressed. We liked each other as people without paying attention to the trappings of success."

"Getting away from it all" appeals to him, and he's toyed with the idea of buying a ranch someplace, cutting his hair short, not worrying about his appearance, and just drawing close to nature. Since his pet peeve on long road tours is the apparent lack of good food and service, he's also considered opening a restaurant to show the world how to combine the two.

If he ever does switch careers, chances are good that he could adjust easily to life out of the spotlight. In spite of the fact that he's one of the most popular performers on one of the most popular shows on TV, he's never had trouble maintaining his equilibrium.

"I've never seen that as a particular problem for me. Ego and pride are human characteristics. Just because I am in front of a lot of people doesn't necessarily mean I have to fight it more than others. I've seen as much pride at church bazaars or potluck suppers when the little lady in the church wants everybody to know that that's *her* pie and *her* recipe and there's none better. Even as Christians there is a part of us that desires glory. But when we start to usurp God's glory, we begin to have real problems."

If Tom doesn't make a drastic change in life styles —and Lawrence Welk fans have their fingers crossed in hopes that he won't—he would like, nevertheless, to improve the quality of his current way of living. He's ambitious and his career will always be important. Yet, since he admits he's put a lopsided emphasis on professional commitments in the past, he's now determined to give equal time to leisure activities and personal relationships.

"I praise God for the growing realization that real living is found in loving and caring relationships and not in fame or wealth. I'm learning that if I want friends I must *be* a friend. I'm trying now to actively cultivate my relationships because I value them and don't want to lose them."

Certainly one popular way for singles to develop relationships is through the many singles' ministries flourishing in today's churches. But Tom's concert schedule makes participation in such a program difficult, and even if he were to come to anchor permanently somewhere, he's not sure he agrees totally with the philosophy of such ministries.

"I felt for the most part that the ones with which I'm familiar are almost like lonely hearts clubs ... a somewhat depressing atmosphere. I got the feeling of 'woe is me' and 'there's no one else so let's all band together.' I think it's wonderful for people with a common interest in life to be able to gather to share with others. The problem is, many times they don't really, honestly share. I don't think a singles' group should be like a summer camp for adults with lots of planned activities. I think it should be geared to turning the attention of its members outward. We don't need to sit around and talk about our loneliness or to find things to entertain and occupy us. We've got to start pouring ourselves into others."

Although he's not actively searching for a mate, he admits he craves the kind of companionship that marriage offers. His first serious love relationship ended abruptly when Tom was called into the Army and his fiancée found someone else in his absence. Today the pain of the experience has dulled and only the lesson he learned remains. He claims he now knows the importance of being sure of his feeling and emotions. Infatuation can easily be mistaken for love, but unlike love, it rarely lasts a lifetime. He's looking for a happily-ever-after kind of relationship with a very special woman.

"First, she needs to be a Christian and someone I enjoy being with as a friend. I've dated some non-Christians and really enjoyed them as people, but there was always something very important missing. I could only develop a close, intimate relationship with a committed Christian.

"Beyond that, she needs to be someone who is honest with her feelings and who has a great sense of humor.

"Romantic love is wonderful, and I like to think of myself as a very romantic person. I love to send flowers or fly to San Francisco for dinner on the spur of the moment. It makes life interesting and helps make the other person feel very special. But romance may change somewhat after marriage. If we are friends and enjoy doing things together, the pressure of romance is eased, and a better climate for a long-lasting relationship is provided."

And a long-lasting relationship—not a string of casual physical encounters—is what interests him. He easily shrugs off the sexual temptations readily presented to any touring nationally known performer. His standards are high, but he has little difficulty adhering to them. He's considered the options and has chosen the refreshingly old-fashioned stance of sex only after the commitment of marriage.

"Sure, the opportunities are there, but they're not a constant temptation. I feel a woman is a person with emotions, feelings, and desires that have to be understood and honored. An affair is a selfish act with no basis of love and with no thought of commitment. I reject that concept. The Bible says love is patient, not self-seeking, always protects, always trusts, always perseveres. I want to be able to exercise that kind of love in dealing with the woman in my life."

He's vocal about these beliefs and, while fans find him exemplary, clean-cut, and the perfect role model for today's young people, skeptics complain that he's too good, untouchable, and squeaky-clean. Surely there must be a wrinkle behind the perfect image he projects.

"I know the Welk show tends to create this image. I always sing a love ballad; seldom speak; never tell a joke or laugh or cry or interact with the audience. But when I go out and do my own shows, I do a variety of things, wear different types of clothes, and show another side of me . . . my real personality.

"I recently showed up for rehearsal in Birmingham

wearing jeans and a T-shirt. A guy looked at me and said, 'Boy, the girls would sure be disappointed if they saw you now.' Another man saw me in Joplin, Missouri, and asked, 'Are you *really* Tom Netherton?' When I assured him I was, he hollered to his wife, 'Come here, honey, it *is* him!' I guess everyone expects me always to be dressed in a suit and tie. I'm just an ordinary person really. I like to dress casually, go barefoot, and eat peanut butter and jelly sandwiches. When I get up in the morning, my hair sticks up in all directions."

But on the Welk show he's perfection personified, and in spite of the image problem it has created, the TV exposure has been good to him. He believes God had a hand in orchestrating the meeting between the champagne king and the gangly young crooner from Minnesota. Why else did Tom just happen to bump into Welk on the putting green of a North Dakota golf course? And why else was he invited to tag along as caddy for a get-acquainted visit between drives, chips, and putts?

"I really believe God has certain things He wants each of us to do in life. The Welk show has been wonderful, but I'm open to the Lord's leading. I've been thinking a lot lately about looking at some new directions. I've even considered going into full-time gospel singing. I want to be where God can use me best. Show business has always been a means to an end for me—the end being, how can I best reach people for Jesus Christ?"

He currently reaches them by sharing his faith verbally and by living as exemplary a life as possible. The two work in tandem, he believes, and he disagrees with persons who lead good, decent lives but reject Christ as their personal Lord and Savior, setting their own standards of righteousness. Equally unacceptable are those who only talk about the Lord but don't live by His Word. To be an effective witness, Tom says, one must be able to deliver the Lord's gift without alienating the recipient.

"Jesus was certainly the perfect example of a gentleman. He would not push Himself on someone who was unreceptive. Christians need to be sensitive people."

He also believes we must be sensitive to God's will for us. When a starring role on a network television show seemed only a signature away, he was pleased but not blinded by the opportunity. When the concept of the show was changed and his role dropped, he accepted without question and was comforted by the belief that God had something else in mind for him. Such flexibility prevents him from setting goals which he may not be able to attain or even wish to pursue.

"Everytime I've set goals, suddenly the goal has become my prime interest. As a Christian I don't want that to happen to me. I want first to be the person God wants me to be. Instead of thinking, 'I want to be on Broadway,' or 'I want to be married by the time I'm thirty-five,' my goals tend to be more general. For instance, I hope I can keep growing and developing my craft to its fullest potential. I hope I can become the very best person that God wants me to be. This leaves the door open for God to do special, surprising, and exciting things with my life."

But surely every performer—even a committed Christian like Tom—dreams of singing on Broadway, starring in his own TV series, and having records high on the charts. He's only human, after all.

"Of course. As an entertainer, Broadway is something I've always thought about doing. And I'd also like to try acting, so I've started taking some lessons. They'll help me succeed in show business. But to help me succeed in life, I don't need drama lessons, voice coaches, bigger audiences, louder applause, truckloads of fan mail, or even fame." He becomes thoughtful for a moment. "To really, really succeed in life," he answers, "I need more of Him and less of me."

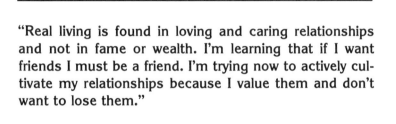

"Real living is found in loving and caring relationships and not in fame or wealth. I'm learning that if I want friends I must be a friend. I'm trying now to actively cultivate my relationships because I value them and don't want to lose them."

Joni Eareckson

The summer after she was voted "Most Athletic Girl" in the graduating class of a suburban Baltimore, Maryland high school, Joni Eareckson broke her neck in a diving accident. Today, though completely paralyzed from the neck down, Joni is a successful commercial artist; author of Joni and A Step Further, having sold over four million copies; and star of a two-million-dollar film version of her life. She has been featured in Time magazine and has appeared on the "Today" show and other national telecasts. Now a resident of California, Joni is director of Joni and Friends, a national ministry providing spiritual and practical advice to those who suffer.

Joni Eareckson

For All Who Suffer

When director Jim Collier yelled "Cut" for the last time on the set of the film *Joni,* a small group of actors quickly shed their characters along with their make-up, scooped up purses and sweaters, and prepared to leave the lush Chesapeake Bay-area horse farm.

The movie was complete. After extensive editing it would be "in the can" awaiting world-wide distribution, and members of the cast were already negotiating new acting assignments. Everyone, that is, except the star.

In the final scene of the film, the camera pulls slowly away and Joni Eareckson's figure grows smaller and smaller against the rolling landscape of the Maryland hills. She sings the background music as the focus blurs to a fadeout and the credits begin to roll. The lights come up and the Hollywood version of Joni's disabling accident, her adaptation to life as a quadriplegic, and the resulting successful ministry, is over. Viewers applaud, make a mental note to recommend it to friends, and then move on to other thoughts. *Great movie! Pizza, anyone?*

But for Joni the drama goes on. The braces that support her arms in the film, the belt that holds her erect, and the wheelchair that gives her mobility aren't props. They have been a way of life for her since 1967—after she dived into the shallow waters of the Chesapeake Bay and snapped her neck. Playing herself in the film was sometimes difficult, often funny, certainly educational, and occasionally downright embarrassing.

"I guess reliving my life before the cameras helped me to relearn, rethink, and reappreciate all the things that I had gone through to bring me to where I am now," says Joni. "On the first day of filming we went to the beach and all I had on was a bathing suit. Well, I hadn't worn a bathing suit at all since my accident, let alone in front of seventy-five people. My corset was wrapped around my swimsuit, my leg bag was hanging out, and my catheter was exposed. I had on an awful wig and no make-up. All of this to re-create an event from my past. But *I* was in the present, sitting in front of all those people, feeling really silly."

For six months she related with cast members, many older than herself, many who didn't share her strong spiritual beliefs. In spite of their differences, the cast and crew became a supportive family.

"Some of them were toughened, hardened, cal- loused professionals—a real contrast to most of the people I had known in my past. But working on the film helped me discover some nice things about myself. I learned that I can get along with many different kinds of people."

Months of convalescence were compacted into min- utes in the film version of Joni's life. But for Joni those minutes opened a floodgate of memories. There was a scene which depicted her heartbreaking realization that she would never ride a horse again; then, the reenactment of the day her favorite mount, Tumbleweed, was led away by his new owner.

"The director, Jim Collier, told me not to wash my hair that morning, but to come to work with it pinned back. I wasn't to put on any make-up and I was supposed to wear a dirty old T-shirt. Suddenly, I remembered how many times I had neglected my appearance in the past. *Since I feel cruddy on the inside,* I thought, *I'm going to look cruddy on the outside.* It brought back some stinging memories, made me grieve for the lost years, and relive the painful months.

If she relived the moments of weakness, she also witnessed an instant replay of her emerging strength. Almost as a bystander, she watched as the film revealed the "old" Joni coming out of her shell of self-pity and resentment.

"I didn't think it would be that real. I thought film-making would be very plastic and very fake, with none of the sights or smells of reality. But the prop masters and director as well as the wardrobe people went to great lengths to recreate a kind of reality.

"When the director called 'Cut' at the end of each shooting session, the actors and actresses could just walk away from the soundstage and go home to normal living. But for me it was difficult to turn off emotions. I'd go home at night telling myself, 'Now, remember, this is just a movie.'" But, of course, it was much more.

Perhaps the film helped deepen her self-awareness and fortify her for a more recent hurt—this one emotional rather than physical. Joni fell in love not long ago, but the relationship wasn't destined to be permanent. Fortunately, neither was the hurt she felt at the time.

"After the heartbreak, my first thought was to go back into the shell. I wanted to bury myself in the Bible, hide myself in my artwork, and devote all my time and attention to my new organization—Joni and Friends. I didn't want to think about close relationships again, but I knew I must fight that tendency. Isolating myself from others would be a giant step backward. Going the 'second mile' would mean continuing to love and be vulnerable. That would really be displaying Christ's love, which keeps giving even when it doesn't get anything in return."

She admits that for too long she refused to believe in her "womanness" because she was struggling with the bolts and bars of a wheelchair. Only within the last two years has she learned to enjoy her single, female state.

"I feel like God has peeled back some layers of my life and cracked the shell. I'm just beginning to enjoy all that it means to be a single woman."

If she's ready for a deep emotional relationship—yes, she hopes to marry someday—she's also aware of the special risks and problems her disability presents. She knows it would take an extraordinary man to cope with her paralysis without smothering her with indulgence or, worse, pity.

"Sometimes men want to be my savior or deliverer. They want to prove their goodness and masculinity by sweeping me off my feet. One man recently said, 'I don't even see the wheelchair.'"

Instead of welcoming the idea that her chair was irrevelant or even invisible, Joni was bothered by it.

"To me, that was a kind of warning signal. I *am* in a wheelchair. I *do* have a disability. I don't always think of it as a handicap because I've learned to adjust and compensate and use my disability to the best of my ability. But when someone doesn't even *see* the chair, then they're just not looking at reality. They haven't even grasped yet what it means to get involved with somebody who's in a wheelchair."

Such an involvement sometimes entails being placed in awkward situations in which modesty must be set aside, with only a sense of humor to bail one out. Joni recalls an afternoon when she and a date went shopping at a nearby mall and suddenly realized her leg bag needed emptying. Her friend couldn't go into the ladies' room and she couldn't enter the men's room. Without warning, she was forced into a predicament that would have been too intimate for a casual acquaintance to handle. Her only recourse in such an uncomfortable moment is accepting her disability and laughing at the unexpected dilemmas it causes.

"I have a sane estimate of my own limitations. I know what is within and what is beyond my reach. Total independence for me is just out of the question; I have to accept the reality that I need someone to help me. Then I feel I can go ahead and work on creating a kind of independence within that perimeter of limitation. The tighter and smaller the framework, the more we are forced to be creative."

Her outlook hasn't always been so healthy. Right after her accident, she struggled with a poor self-image. All the yardsticks she had used in measuring her life were meaningless when she became a quadriplegic. How fast she could ride a horse, how well she could swim, how far she could run no longer contributed to her sense of worth. A new set of standards had to be devised.

"I had to work out a proper self-image concerning the preciousness of my soul in God's eyes. I had to believe that God was going to do some lovely things in my life, thereby making me a lovely person. At first, this thought was repulsive to me because I didn't love God and I didn't feel lovely. I just wanted to strike out in pain and hurt. When I got out of the hospital my life started going upward, but the rejection from my boyfriend at that time had been like a pair of scissors that had snipped away from my self-image that part of me that was a pretty woman. It hurt and I didn't want to be hurt again."

For singles who have experienced the pain of rejection, Joni urges them not to look back, but to accept the circumstances and trust that God knows best. This may be difficult, she admits, but in the end new strength comes out of the struggle. In her unhappiest moments she repeated over and over, "This too will pass. God will take care of me."

Still, Joni is human. She suffers periods of loneliness and, like everyone else, sometimes she cries. When she turned thirty and realized she was financially independent, she moved cross-continent from Maryland to southern California. Her sister Jay, who had cared for her ten years, was planning to be married, and Joni wanted to give her space to start a family of her own. California seemed a likely choice for relocation because of the warm climate and her many friends there. But though the move was exciting, homesickness struck, most often on holidays.

"One Thanksgiving my sister, Kathy, came out to visit me and as we sat around the table we bowed our heads to say grace. At the end of the prayer she said, *Lord, I thank You for my loving sister.* It took all my strength to keep from crying because, all at once, in a flood of emotion, I missed my family. Then I stopped and counted my blessings and remembered I am here by God's providence. I am living the life He wants me to live right now. To put it simply, I'm wedged in His will—and that helps."

Sometimes the tears can't be checked. She wants to go off by herself and cry herself dry, but she can't. Even moments of solitude have to be planned.

She's candid about her "down" moods and wants admirers to be aware that she suffers depression, discouragement, and disappointment. She refuses to be put upon a pedestal and cringes when fans treat her like some kind of idol. She's not, and is the first to admit it.

"People assume that I am a woman of great courage and extraordinary faith because I can live adequately without the use of my hands and legs. Well, I am by no stretch of anyone's imagination a strong person. I don't have the kind of constitution it takes to live in a wheelchair. All this proves that it has to be God's grace. Paul refers to our bodies as earthen vessels. My earthen vessel is certainly made of weak and crumbling clay. If I handle it well it's only by the grace of God, not by my courage."

The circle of her limitations is gradually being enlarged. After extensive evaluation, a doctor at California State University determined that with special instruction, training, and equipment Joni would be able to drive a van alone. The vehicle, purchased for her ministry by the church she attends, is customized in the full sense of the word. She can wheel her chair up into the driver's alcove and be locked into position automatically. Through a number of buttons she can start the engine; then, thanks to a special stick, she can accelerate, steer, and stop the vehicle.

On the day of her test drive she was ecstatic with anticipation. The responsibility of making such simple decisions as stopping at yield signs and turning corners seemed challenging and deliriously rewarding.

"That might seem difficult to understand for people who drive every day," she says. "But for someone who used to drive a sports car and then couldn't get behind a steering wheel for twelve years, it's thrilling."

Such victories are sweet, because Joni knows some obstacles can never be surmounted. Sometimes, when she thinks too long or too hard about her future and her ever-present limitations, she feels claustrophobic. The sensation of not being able to move is frightening, especially when she knows it's permanent. Occasionally, she admits, she wishes time away, anticipating the promise of wholeness after death. She dreams of enjoying her new, heavenly body.

"But that's when heaven becomes an escape, a cop-out, a psychological crutch. I never want to use the hope of heaven in that way. I want my heavenly perspective to influence my earthly perspective . . . enjoying what God is going to do through me now. Then my longing for heaven will not be an escape but a healthy hope."

Perhaps the biggest battle she fights is against giving in to a kind of all-consuming self-centeredness. She claims she doesn't want to become so taken up with "me, myself, and I" thoughts that she doesn't have time for others. She recognizes this as a problem many disabled—and single—people face.

Often handicapped persons are selfish, she admits. When she struggles through bouts with self-pity, she tries to look at her own circumstances in light of somebody else who is also struggling.

"Sometimes we think our situation is beyond comparison. We think that God's grace can be appropriated for every other individual except for ourselves. If we just take the time to look at others who are hurting, our problems won't seem so big. I have several friends who are disabled, actually far more severely than I am, and just to look at their perseverance and endurance, to see how their loyalty shines through is an encouragement to me."

Constant communication with God helps too. And, she stresses, it must be a two-way dialogue. She communicates with God through prayer and He communicates with her through the Bible. No matter how demanding her schedule, she always sets aside time for prayer and Bible study.

She realizes that in several ways she's far more fortunate than most disabled persons. The success of her artwork and books has enabled her to become financially independent. The purchase of her home was a move she views as another step forward in her growth process. The choice of owning property was her own and so are the responsibilities.

"Buying new furniture is the fun part. The mortgage payments aren't. I've added a fashionable oak headboard to my hospital bed so that you wouldn't recognize it."

More independence has done a lot for Joni's self-image, but she refuses to become caught up in her own achievements or acquisitions. She constantly keeps in mind her scores of friends whose disabilities confine them to nursing homes or convalescent centers. She knows many do not have the family support, the friends, and finances that she enjoys.

"I am truly, truly blessed," she says. "That is not to say my friends in rehab centers or convalescent homes don't enjoy their lives. God gives them the grace to be where they are and that's a special and wonderful thing. I know that if I weren't in this position and if I had to live in a nursing home, God would give me that grace too."

Joni is concerned that her disabled friends who can't be visibly active in the community are too often forgotten or ignored. Even the church is guilty of neglect, she says. One idea she heartily endorses is removing a few pews so the disabled person can be mainstreamed into the congregation rather than having to sit apart, in the aisle or at the back of the church. She dislikes the label "handi-capped" and prefers to be referred to as "a young woman with a disability." After all, she is first of all a person.

Educating churches and individuals to the needs of disabled persons is just one of the purposes of her new organization—Joni and Friends. Termed "a ministry to those who suffer," the group will offer help to persons who are trying to deal with spiritual and mental problems as well as physical handicaps. Those who have experi-enced the loss of a mate through death or divorce also suffer and Joni wants to touch their lives, too, through her ministry.

"People write to me every day with questions that run the gamut from spiritual needs to practical information. For instance: 'What does the Bible say about suffering, miracles, and healing?' 'How do I cope with depression?' 'Where do I find the best hospitals or rehab centers?' 'What about new equipment and treatments that are available?' 'What colleges are suitable for handicapped people?' 'What kinds of scholarships are possible?'

"Because handicaps and disabilities come in all shapes and sizes, we attempt to meet as many needs and answer as many questions as possible. We want to reach the young person who suffers from multiple sclerosis, the person who has lost a mate, and the housewife on the verge of a nervous breakdown."

Such disabilities—mental, physical, and spiritual— may sound extreme, but Joni doesn't believe a person must suffer the depths of despair before he can experience the heights of joy. Pain and hurt are not prerequisites to spirituality.

"God deals with us in many different ways. But I believe for those of us who do experience the depths of despair, the heights of joy become all the sweeter and more precious . . . to the point where we not only find our suffering agreeable, but at times can even rejoice in it. I believe that suffering figures into the whole redemption story. There's no fine print in the contract. I think writers of the New Testament make it clear that if we sign up in the army of Christ, we're going to receive some bumps and bruises."

She feels the "bumps and bruises" entailed in the Christian life may increase in the decade of the eighties because of the controversial issues on which Christians must take a stand. Social questions such as abortion and euthanasia trouble her. She believes they signal a morality change in the United States and she fears that Christians who speak out against the trend may face persecution and suffering.

"I think Christians are going to experience some suffering according to the will of God in this decade. At the beginning of every year I choose a Bible verse to use as a guideline for the following months. For this year, even for this decade, I selected this verse: 'Those who suffer according to God's will should commit themselves to their faithful Creator and continue to do good' (1 Pet. 4:19 NIV). In our country today many people tend to think of life as less and less precious. As Christians we have to fight that tendency. I think we're called on to trust and obey Him. I stand firm on these issues and I speak clearly about the preciousness of life and God's love for us."

Her high visibility—the film, her books, frequent appearances on secular TV talk shows—provides her with a platform to speak her mind and share her views. If she has one thought she likes to pass on via the various media now open to her, it has to do with stretching up to God rather than pulling God down to human levels.

"It's the whole idea of not letting our suffering diminish our view of our great and glorious God. Sometimes, when we hurt, we tend to pull God down to our level, demanding that He be accountable to us. We must be careful to maintain a high view of God. He is not accountable to us. He never needs to explain Himself. He did enough explaining on the cross. That makes Him worthy of our trust and love."

She sees this as a vital message for Christians to remember as they cope with problems and possible persecution in the future. However great the suffering, Joni believes it shouldn't detract from the sufferer's focus on God. Neither should it lessen his love and responsibility for persons around him—especially those whose burden is even heavier.

"What's the old adage? 'I grumbled and complained because I had no shoes until I met a man who had no feet.' If we just consider the bleeding body of Christ, then I think we will take our eyes off ourselves and turn them toward serving, helping, and encouraging others."

"God deals with us in many different ways. But I believe for those of us who do experience the depths of despair, the heights of joy become all the sweeter and more precious . . . to the point where we not only find our suffering agreeable, but at times can even rejoice in it. I believe that suffering figures into the whole redemption story."

Harold Ivan Smith

Harold Ivan Smith, whose pseudonym is Jason Towner, holds degrees from Trevecca Nazarene College, Scarritt College, and George Peabody College of Vanderbilt University, all in Nashville. Formerly a college administrator, he is presently serving as the first general director of single adult ministries for the Church of the Nazarene, Kansas City, Missouri. The author of three books and numerous articles appearing in religious publications, he travels across the nation conducting conferences and seminars on pertinent issues confronting single adults.

Jason Towner

After the Tears

Harold Ivan Smith—Christian college graduate, active member of an evangelical church, once devoted husband —had known his divorce papers were coming, of course. Counseling had been attempted and discarded, long talks had ensued and failed, friends had interceded and given up. It was all over but the crying. Still, the routine act of accepting the legal papers when they were served was so traumatic, so final, that years later the pain of the moment recurs with the memory.

"The doors were all open," he recalls. "I tried to hold back the tears as long as I could, but there was this welling up in my chest. The tears had to be vocal as well as visual. Looking back, I know it was okay. I just wish somebody had told me then that it was all right to cry."

The marriage had failed slowly and quietly, without shrill exchanges and with no single, divisive issue. Lines of communication simply clogged, feelings eroded, and the chasm gradually became too wide to bridge. A year of marriage counseling came too late. Jane didn't love her husband anymore and no amount of counseling or praying could change that. The last fifteen months of their marriage were spent trying to resuscitate the lifeless relationship. Finally, she moved out.

"We stopped communicating. I don't mean we stopped talking to each other; we never fought or yelled or fussed. That wasn't our thing," he says. "But somehow the couple who had once sat for hours on a swing in Centennial Park in Nashville, planning the future, stopped sharing dreams."

Other problems surfaced. The physical aspect of marriage fell short of their expectations. Jane had difficulty responding sexually to her husband. Harold blamed himself and felt as if he had somehow failed as a mate. The topic was too sensitive for words, so they silently decided to ignore it in the hope the problem would disappear. It didn't.

"We were always too busy or too tired to talk. I was an associate pastor of a church and a student in graduate school. The only time we had for each other was Saturday morning between trips to the grocery and chores around the house. We began postponing things. We'd say, 'Let's wait till the end of the semester to talk about that,' or 'After my exam we'll think about this.'"

Eventually there was nothing to think about, to say, or more importantly, to dream. First came divorce and then the tears.

"I cried far longer than I should have had to cry. My grief could have been less, but people who had endured the same experience wouldn't talk to me about it. God doesn't comfort us just so we can be 'cool' singles, but so we can share that comfort with somebody else. 'We can pass on to them the same help and comfort God has given us'" (2 Cor. 1:4 LB).

He looked to his church for solace and found a neglected singles' group which had always been dismissed as a gathering of spinster schoolteachers who ate together at Morrison's Cafeteria. Now he was one of them. After the tears subsided, concern set in.

"Why isn't the church interested in singles? On Sunday evening—a particularly tough time for singles—why don't couples in the church invite unmarried members home after the service? The Lord finally tired of hearing my questions and replayed some 'video tapes' of my past. In six years of marriage Jane and I had never once invited a single to our home on Sunday night. I had planted no seeds, yet now that I was divorced, I expected the harvest."

The Smiths hadn't intentionally ignored singles, but they had never been taught how to minister to them. The classes they had taken in college didn't focus on the divorced person, widows, widowers, or other persons living solo. They were unacquainted with the special problems faced by persons living alone, and they were unsure of singles' needs and hurts. Harold decided the church had been geared for so long to the family unit that it wasn't certain how to address people outside the unit, especially those who had been married and were now alone.

"Nobody knows quite what to say. I guess that's why Hallmark doesn't make divorce cards . . . there's no pat message or little verse. When it comes to divorce we let people drift along, and it shouldn't be that way. Somehow we need to reach out and help them."

Recognizing the shortcoming was one thing, but knowing how to correct it was another. What could he do to prevent others from crying for as long as he had cried? How could he ease their pain? To find the solution he first scrutinized the situation, dissecting it and analyzing it against the backdrop of his own experience. He looked back to his student days when he and Jane began their married life like so many of their friends, "playing house" in a tiny on-campus apartment. That's where the problems had begun.

"There is a saying that if marriages are made in heaven, then Christian colleges are branch offices. For some parents it's worth the price of tuition alone to send their kids to a Christian school because they're likely to meet Mr. or Miss Right there. But the marriage factor should be the last concern of a church-affiliated school. We need to be preparing people for responsible stewardship in the kingdom. If marriage comes, that's great. But what happens if Mr. Right isn't so right after all? The divorce rate among Christian college students is astounding."

Besides overemphasizing the mating game, Christian colleges tend to ignore married students, according to Harold. As singles, he and Jane had been considered "kids." Once married, they were instantly adults on their own. Nothing was done by the faculty or administration to keep the union solvent. No aid was available to bolster a marriage that buckled under the burdens of financial problems, scholastic pressures, fatigue, and general adjustment difficulties. No classes were offered to prepare married students for their new life.

He looked farther back, to the time when he and Jane and many of their friends were planning weddings and attending pastoral conferences in preparation for the ceremonies. Too often these sessions amounted to one brief meeting at the church to decide who stands where.

"Some pastors are finally getting serious about premarital counseling and are requiring batteries of psychological tests for couples wanting to get married. Five and six counseling sessions are expected and if the couple doesn't attend all of them, the minister won't perform the ceremony. I'm for it. The church is going to have to become more responsible. I think the day is coming when a pastor may even be sued for negligence if he marries some couples. Occasionally I hear ministers say they refuse to marry divorced people. They'll marry anyone the first time around, but no one the second time. There should be one standard. If people need a church ceremony the first time, they need it even more the second time."

The church had some catching up to do, he decided. Not only must divorce be accepted as an unhappy but very real phenomenon, but the church has a certain obligation to help singles rebuild their lives after divorce. This rebuilding process must include guidance during the healing process and sustained support as the problems of single life are encountered. He recognized that some people simply do not feel complete unless they are married. But too often a single will plunge into a second relationship as soon as he or she experiences warm, fuzzy feelings toward someone. Again, counseling is needed to sort out emotions and prevent, if necessary, a second marriage which is surely destined for an unhappy ending.

Harold felt he could help. As a minister, he was a trained counselor who knew the Scriptures and could apply and interpret them. As a divorced man, he had firsthand knowledge of the needs and hurts shared by survivors of broken marriages. He saw where the church fell short and he wanted to help correct that shortcoming. He would start with a book, he decided, based on the failure of his marriage. Perhaps by telling the story of his own divorce, he could help others who faced the pain he knew so well.

But there was a problem. The editor of the Christian publishing house which was interested in his book felt uncomfortable about using Harold's real name on it. He and Jane were separated at the time and the book could have possibly become a barrier to a reconciliation. A pen name seemed the solution. But what name?

"Jane and I had always said we would name our first

son after Dr. Walter Towner, a college professor who helped me understand the gospel in an expansive, compassionate way. We liked 'Jason' better than 'Walter' for some reason, but we promised Dr. Towner someday there would be a Jason Towner Smith. As I found myself midway through divorce proceedings I knew, of course, there would never be a Jason Towner in our marriage; but still, perhaps the name could survive as a symbol of hope."

The "birth" of Jason Towner, author, also marked the birth of a vital singles' ministry. By helping others, Jason found his own healing was accelerated. His book, *Jason Loves Jane (But They Got a Divorce),* acquainted readers with the author, whom they quickly accepted as one from their own ranks. Other people might preach or lecture about divorce, but here was a man who had lived it and knew it inside out.

The next step was for Jason to go on the road and meet the readers who already considered him a sympathetic friend. Weekend singles' seminars brought together a broad mixture of singles. The common denominator for a large percentage of them was the fact they had all endured divorce. Everyone benefited from the candid, give-and-take discussions. Everyone, including Jason.

"My healing obligates me to share with other people. I want to see if I can help reduce the number of weeks or months that people have to cry. An encourager is needed during the healing process. Some people really pick at the scabs, but there comes a time when you have to trust the scabs to the Lord. I look at my life today and I can't believe the scars aren't any more noticeable."

A few persons who attend his seminars claim they are offended by his frankness. While he stresses that perpetual adultery is surely grounds for divorce, a single act of unfaithfulness, however harmful to a relationship, can be forgiven by a spouse who is committed to the growth of the marriage. And remember, he cautions, just because a husband or wife may have grounds for divorce doesn't mean he or she has grounds for remarriage.

"I think there are three criteria for remarriage: One, have you forgiven your ex *and* yourself? Two, have you allowed enough time to heal the wounds caused by divorce? Three, do you believe it is God's will for you to enter into this second marriage?"

He talks about intimacy, the Christian discipline of no sexual relations outside marriage, and his own personal commitment to celibacy.

"Some people seem to have the notion that the sexual experience is a lot like a cassette recorder. After divorce, you hit the stop button, then push the rewind button, go back to zero and start all over again—this time, hopefully, without pimples. But it's not that easy, and this is a crucial point the church has ignored. It's one thing for a person who has never been sexually involved to say no to intimacy. It's something else for someone to say no who is familiar with the script, who knows how to get from A to B to C expediently and easily. A person who has never been that route isn't sure of all the steps in between."

While some persons may be so hurt by the divorce experience that they feel no desire for intimacy, ultimately there comes a moment when their sexual needs resurface and must be recognized. For Jason, it was a painful process because he felt deprived.

"Even though our sexual relationship was not perfect, I'd be wrong to say I don't miss it. But I believe it's a question of discipline. Celibacy is a difficult, demanding standard. I'm celibate outside marriage because Christ asks me to be. He was celibate and faced the same issues that I face. He expects me to follow His example. That's why He died as an adult. He could have died as an infant in the manger and His blood would have saved us. But He died as an adult so He could fully understand what we experience as adults."

Temptations are frequent, especially on the seminar circuit. Often people attend the sessions not so much for guidance but to meet other singles like themselves who might be interested in a relationship. Almost inevitably a woman attempts to walk off with the grand prize—the seminar leader. Jason knows this and avoids blending his professional and private lives. He must be totally believable to people if they are to trust him. This means no games, no double standards—just honesty and straight-from-the-hip dialogue.

"The day I start playing games with people in seminars is the day I'll hang it up and do something else. The irony is that some people want to date Jason Tower who wouldn't want to go out with Harold Smith. But Jason doesn't date and Harold does. There's a difference."

Since Jason is his "public" personality and Harold is his private side, one can study the other with a certain amount of detachment. Before Jason launched his ministry, he took stock of Harold's appearance and decided it wasn't in tune with the message of total Christian discipline which "both" advocated. How could people respect him and listen to his advice when he weighed in at a hefty 275 pounds? Jason issued an ultimatum to Harold: Eighty pounds had to go.

"The crazy thing is that I had always believed Jane accepted me the way I was at 275 pounds. My first excursion into the world of singles taught me that no one else did. The weight definitely had to go. Quite frankly, I can't imagine a fat Jesus!"

Harold's doctor lectured him about his weight. How could he refrain from drinking, smoking, and being promiscuous on the grounds they were sinful acts, yet not recognize as sin 10,000 calories worth of food a day?

"God gave you the right to be born in America," scolded the doctor, "but not the right to eat calories that belong to some kid in India!"

He had to find a diet that worked for him—yogurt and carrot curls just weren't on his list of favorite snacks. By eating slowly once a day and choosing foods he craved, but in moderate portions, he began to drop pounds. He philosophized as he dieted and concluded that singles are more tempted to overeat than couples.

"You sit around with no one to talk to, munching on whatever's handy. If there's one piece of pie left over from dinner, you don't have to save it for anyone. And who's going to tell you not to eat the whole bag of potato chips? You can be as fat as you want. No one's watching."

As he lost weight, he gained confidence. Suddenly it was fun to buy clothes. He added jogging to his daily schedule and the pounds melted away more quickly. His morning run soon became a time of spiritual as well as physical exercise.

"That is the time I commune with the Lord. People ask how I can pray while I run. It's easy. While my body is moving at maximum speed, my whole system is go. I used to roll out of bed, slide to the floor on my knees, and say, *O God, give me the strength to get into the shower so I can wake up.* Now I run through the park before it is polluted with noise. I watch the sun come up and enjoy nature the way God must see it."

The weight-reduction program continues even now that he's achieved his goal of 195 pounds. He claims he feels the Lord nudging him and urging him to keep to his regimen. He's convinced the day is coming when God will no longer continue to let Americans eat the way we do while Christian brothers go hungry.

"We ought to have discipline in everything, yet in our society *discipline* is a negative word. Look at the way we eat, spend our money, abuse our credit cards."

He has always stressed self-discipline in his singles seminars, but now his neat appearance underscores his words. He's trim, athletic-looking, and well-groomed. "People expect a speaker to look good. This is as much a ministry as if I were pastoring a church," he says.

His conservative appearance—short hair and three-piece suit—adds credibility to his no-holds-barred beliefs which he expounds during singles' seminars. He speaks honestly about the tendency of some churches to over-burden members with church-related obligations. His listeners, who may not entirely agree with him, are at least willing to hear his message.

"We have pastors who reemphasize that people should get involved. Sometimes I wonder if the church doesn't cause some divorces by taking so much time from the family. I'm not talking about spiritual obligations, but rather the extra activities that can wear people out. We need to spend more time, quiet time, with our mates and our families."

He condones divorce in certain situations. This stance causes some conservative churchgoers to cringe. They argue that as the church accepts divorce, the divorce rate increases.

"There have always been and always will be a lot of unhappy marriages in the church," says Harold. "I don't believe God gets a thing out of marriages that are stuck together only to fight like a couple we called the Battling Baxters. The Baxters were a couple who were married twenty-five years and fought every Saturday night. Their kids despised marriage and saw nothing good in it. The Baxters are still 'pillars of the church' although everyone knows their marriage is not an enriching experience. Their children might have been hurt by a divorce, but they have been permanently injured by a marriage that is far less than God wants."

Unlike some pastors, he sees no conflict between a

strong emphasis on marriage and an equally strong emphasis on a ministry to singles. The goal of both is the same—helping people to become what God wants them to be. The stress should be on achieving wholeness.

"We have this notion that we become complete when we get married. The Bible teaches us we become complete when we become Christians. Marriage should be a union of two complete persons, not two halves. We are each whole in Jesus Christ."

This is the message he carries on the road, weekend after weekend, throughout the country. He tells about his personal walk with loneliness and insecurity and explains how, with God's help, he has worked through the troubled times. He doesn't speak in platitudes or hazy generalities, but in specifics. He knows how it feels to eat Easter Sunday dinner in a fast-food restaurant, face a three-day weekend without any plans, have an exciting bit of news to tell—but no one to tell it to.

"Openness and honesty are the key elements in my seminars," he says. "Why not be candid and talk about problems and get help by dialoguing? My feeling is that people pay to attend a singles' seminar to hear something solid they can take home with them for review. I have seen burdens lifted. I've seen people walk out of a seminar with their backs straight for the first time in months. I can't carry their backpacks for them, but if I can help rearrange some things and help them get rid of excess baggage, then I have contributed to them."

But at the end of each seminar, Jason Towner, lecturer, becomes Harold Smith again, who has to deal with his own problems. Living a suitcase life style isn't all glamour and excitement. After a while one city looks like the next, the hotel food tastes the same, and the trip home is always long.

"For me, Sunday night is the toughest—when I fly back home to Kansas City, get into my Volkswagen and drive to my apartment. I've been in the limelight and I've been treated royally. Suddenly I'm just a John Doe—and a lonely one at that. No one is waiting to meet me at the airport and say, 'Harold, I'm really glad you're home.' I'd like to open the door to my apartment in the evening and hear, 'Hey, how'd it go?' And on holidays I wish there were someone to say, 'Merry Christmas, Harold Ivan Smith.'"

Someday there may be a "someone" again for him ... someone who will love and accept both Jason and Harold and recognize them as one and the same. In the meantime, he will continue to minister, to help others, and in so doing, to help himself. That's enough for now.

"I hope that spring will follow winter, but I'm not sure of that. All I know is that the Lord calls me to an abundant, full life as a single. He doesn't guarantee that I will live to be sixty-five. I have today, and I have to live it as positively, as fully, and as redemptively as I can. The Lord has a plan for me. I don't know if that plan includes a mate or not, but I know that it is not second best. If I am obedient to what He has for me, He will fill in the details."

"We have this notion that we become complete when we get married. The Bible teaches us we become complete when we become Christians. Marriage should be a union of two complete persons, not two halves. We are each whole in Jesus Christ."

Keith and Andrea Miller

*A*ndrea Wells Miller, *a graduate of Furman University, and Keith Miller, who holds degrees from the University of Oklahoma; Berkeley Divinity School, New Haven; Earlham School of Religion, Richmond, Indiana; and the University of Texas, were married in February 1979.*

Together, they have produced a study course entitled Faith, Intimacy, and Risk in the Single Life *and a book,* The Single Experience. *He is the author of eight additional books, and she, of* The Choir Director's Handbook. *Mrs. Miller formerly served as Director of Marketing for the Music Division of Word, Inc. An oil-entrepreneur-turned-author, Keith Miller is in great demand as lecturer, counselor, and business consultant. The Millers currently fill an extensive schedule of speaking engagements and seminars.*

Keith and Andrea Miller
Our Single Season

Keith and Andrea Miller had two things in common the day they met—each had watched a happy marriage disintegrate into utter failure, and each was determined never to make *that* mistake again.

They were also intent upon building something—he, a writing and counseling career; she, a career and a new identity. Why not? She was feeling strong and independent, exploring facets of her personality she didn't know existed. So was he.

After dating each other exclusively for a year, they felt themselves attracted to the idea of remarriage. Since they both had reservations, however, they submitted to the ultimate test. They decided to stop seeing each other for three months. Ninety long days.

"We struggled with the idea of getting married," says Keith. "We both had been hurt once, *and* we were concerned about the big difference in our ages. So, after dating for a lengthy period, we separated for ninety days. I felt that we just couldn't marry without a lot of careful thought and prayer. It occurred to me that if I did re-marry, it might mean the end of my public career. But I also thought that it would be phony not to do what I believed was right for me just to avoid disturbing people. It would be a denial of everything I've tried to say."

After her divorce, Andrea had flatly announced she would never marry again ". . . as long as I feel the way I do now." She simply wasn't cut out for it, she told her friends, and she now felt there was a better way to make a break with parents than to jump from the sheltered atmosphere of her parental home to the similar security offered by a husband. Looking back, she asked, "What was the big rush anyway?"

"I was married the first time at twenty-two, without knowing who I was, much less whom I was marrying. I wish I hadn't felt such a social stigma about waiting until I was older to marry. And I wish I had approached a career as if it were the way I was going to live for the rest of my life, instead of thinking, *It doesn't matter what kind of job I get because I'm going to get married anyway.*"

She recalls spending her "terrible twenties" being more concerned about the questions of her first husband's willingness to keep their apartment tidy than exploring her own identity and learning to communicate with her husband. Three years later that marriage was in trouble. And after a year of counseling in an attempt to bridge the communications gap, the marriage failed. As Andrea embarked on a crash course in getting to know herself, she found that being single was hardly the completely unhappy state she had feared.

"The years I spent single were definitely some of the most exciting times of my life in terms of growth. It was like being on the roller coaster at Six Flags. I had some ups and downs and turnarounds, but I found out a lot about who I am. I was free to explore sides of myself I didn't know existed. I even did mechanical things like building a stereo AM/FM receiver from a kit. And it works! The single life has its hard, difficult, miserable times, but there are a lot of aspects about it that I liked and that benefited me."

Keith returned to single life via a different route. A well-known Christian writer and speaker, he had struggled to make his marriage work. He sought help by joining a counseling group as a participant rather than in his customary role as leader. When divorce was inevitable, he moved to another community to start a new life.

"I spent a lot of time alone before I began to date," he recalls. "Dating was really strange for me—I felt like a young boy again. My pride and masculinity were on the line. The role of the single was different from thirty years ago. I wasn't even in the same world. I had a lot to find out about myself."

Looking back on the mistakes of his first marriage, he realized he had been unprepared for a permanent relationship. Like Andrea, he didn't really know who he was when he assumed the responsibilities of a spouse. He thinks a counseling group might have helped him *before* marriage to identify his goals and fears. It might have caused him to face what he calls "the whole business of being intimate."

"You may say, 'Well, that's ridiculous for a Christian.' But I think we Christians *especially* need this because so often we are taught to hide our feelings. If one comes to know himself, at least he brings one whole person into the marriage, thereby giving it a 50 percent chance for success. Even if one never marries, he can experience life in a fuller way by knowing more about himself and the person God wants him to be."

Keith and Andrea met after he had been divorced for one year and she, for four years. With one other person, they formed a small Christian prayer group for the purpose of talking and praying in depth about each other's lives. Andrea and Keith were stunned by the similarity of their needs. Without a marriage on which to blame their problems, both were determined to learn more about themselves and their niches in life.

"I had never met any woman who was on the same search for authenticity and intimacy as I," says Keith. "I always tried to out-intimacy everybody, but I couldn't do that with Andrea, because she's so honest. She wanted Jesus Christ and honesty as much as I did. It was threatening. I learned I wasn't as far along on this integrity trip as I had assumed."

As for Andrea, she quickly learned never to say "never" again. Her assurances that marriage "was fine for other people but not for me, thanks" no longer sounded convincing. She began to re-examine her goals and question her aversion to a deep relationship.

"I began to see it was not my place to say what I would 'never' do again because of my past experiences. But it *was* my place to open my mind and heart to learn what God wanted me to do. I had all kinds of reasons for not wanting to think about remarriage. I didn't think anybody could stand my need for honesty. I didn't think anybody could handle a lot of things I wanted out of life. Later, I decided I was wrong; perhaps I could better be what God wanted me to be by marrying again."

Deciding to divorce and then choosing to remarry were probably the greatest acts of faith Keith has ever undertaken. He knew the statement in Matthew 19:9, that anyone divorcing his wife and marrying another commits adultery. But as he read through the Bible, he saw that the degree of condemnation toward divorce that is found in some churches today *isn't* found in the Scriptures! He saw Jesus as One who continually gave people new life and new chances after they had failed (*e.g.,* the Prodigal Son, the woman at the well, the woman caught in the act of adultery, *et al*). He prayed: *Lord, I've got to trust You to be even bigger than they say You are.* He staked his future, and Andrea staked hers, too, on the belief that Christ's forgiveness is greater than rules.

"I'm not trying to excuse divorce or say it's not wrong. I'm just saying that the God of the New Testament, walking around in Jesus Christ, was *much* bigger than the rules He gave. His actions showed this again and again. Jesus and His disciples broke the Sabbath by picking and eating corn. *He* said the Sabbath was made for man, not man for the Sabbath.

"When Jesus made the statement about divorce in Matthew 19, it was as if He were reaching up into the moral night, poking stars into the heavens. We can look at those stars and chart our course through life, even though in our humanity we can never reach the perfection of the stars themselves. He taught with those kinds of absolutes, knowing we cannot keep them. If we could, we wouldn't need the forgiveness we claim He died to give."

Before making their final decision to marry, Keith and Andrea talked with a counselor, first separately and then together. They wanted to know what obstacles they faced and what the counselor might see in their relationship that could cause problems after marriage. The feedback was positive—they were told they were one of the best communicating couples he had ever seen.

With this added assurance, they were married in a unique ceremony which they wrote themselves. Having read the services from *The Book of Common Prayer* and a Presbyterian service, they paraphrased the essentials in more colloquial English. They memorized the vows and repeated them without prompting from the minister. Only twenty-eight persons were invited to hear the exchange of promises.

"I wanted to say to all of our family and friends who were there what I intended to do and what my promise to

Keith was," recalls Andrea. "I wanted to say it not just before God and the minister, but before my mother, father, sisters, brother, aunts, uncles, and all the other people who knew about my past failures and my new decision."

"In the vows," adds Keith, "I said that I would help Andrea become all that she could become under God. In an intimate relationship we are often so vulnerable that we can either cripple or create conditions for amazing growth and change. Andrea and I believe that, and we asked God to help us to help each other grow in His way."

Although they didn't realize it at the time, their experiences would also help others to grow—especially persons who struggle with the dilemmas of divorce and remarriage. Instead of ending Keith's public career, as he once feared, their marriage opened up a bigger, broader ministry to them. They knew firsthand the pain of marital failure and were willing to share what they had felt and learned via their books, lectures, and tapes. Whenever called upon to speak on the divorce issue, they are quick to deal with any feelings of guilt. They realize some Christians may feel condemned by God because they have failed at marriage. Andrea deals with her own feelings about this by her belief that, if a person makes a mistake and confesses it to God, it's as if He takes a damp cloth and wipes the blackboard clean. The person is then free to begin again to write the next chapter of his or her life.

Based on the considerable amount of marriage counseling he has done, Keith adds further support to the argument that divorce is not an unpardonable sin.

"If a Christian can't sin and be forgiven, then Paul wasn't a Christian," stresses Keith. "Paul said, 'I'm the chief of sinners' and he really meant it. The closer we get to Jesus Christ, the more we see how we are not like Him.

The more sinful things we see about our own humanity, the more we say, 'No, *I'm* the chief of sinners.' The one who has really sinned and repented understands sin better. The church seems to want perfect leaders, yet Jesus said, 'I can't even help you if you don't understand that you need a physician' (paraphrasing Matt. 9:12). The Bible says Jesus ran around with sinners and, when He was criticized for it by the Pharisees, He replied in effect, 'It is these sinners that I have come to save.'"

Keith emphasizes that people who hold a marriage together merely out of a legalistic fear of God cannot be credited with great Christian motive. And then there are the ministers and church lay leaders who often spend too much time rushing around trying to prevent divorce "at all costs." A more constructive approach might be for the ministers to help when possible, but to try to become the role models for couples in their congregations by staying home with their mates and working on their own marriages. Too often pastors and other people view marital difficulties as some kind of weakness or shortcoming on the part of the spouses. In reality, Keith believes, *everyone is vulnerable to problems—yes, even church leaders themselves.*

"Our leaders have to start providing honest, open role models so that together we can begin dealing with our shortcomings in a healthy way. For example, if a minister were to be able to say, 'My wife and I have had real problems in our marriage and this is the way we're learning to face them together,' rather than, 'Praise the Lord! We always have the victory!' we could all breathe a sigh of relief. If we could have a good, solid model of an intimate marriage, people may begin to enjoy and grow in marriage again. Jesus set for us the best example of intimacy by being open and vulnerable with His own life. Our best bet is to start living what we're preaching and start learning how to be intimate."

When counseling couples contemplating marriage, Keith and Andrea stress the importance of open closeness as an essential ingredient in a happy relationship. Many people think intimacy is synonymous with sexuality. The Millers see the open closeness of intimacy as a prerequisite to healthy and fulfilling sexuality.

"Intimacy is the relationship in which a person is safe to express his or her real feelings, hopes, dreams, fears, guilts, and sins without the fear of judgment or condemnation," says Keith. "A trusting closeness is the essential thing. Sex in marriage is the sacrament of intimacy . . . the outward and visible sign of the inward spiritual intimacy. Intimacy is present when each is inside the other's life. And in sexual intercourse we are actually designed so that at the most intimate moment of our lives, when we are creating new life as man and woman, we are physically inside each other's lives—a superb symbol of intimacy.

"In a similar way, the sacraments in the church are the outward signs of a life of confession, forgiveness, and continuous communication with God. The sacraments can be boring if the confession, forgiveness, and communication aren't going on inside the participant. If real intimacy doesn't develop in a relationship, people often go directly to sex, wrongly believing that sex *is* intimacy. But authentic sex, it seems to me, doesn't happen until after intimacy is established."

How can two people approach the kind of intimacy that Keith describes? First, each partner must be willing to face head-on his or her own inadequacies, fears, hates, and negative thoughts, instead of trying to repress them. Repression occurs when we push our unacceptable thoughts into the unconscious part of our minds. It's like trying to hold a beach ball under water. It takes a great deal of psychological energy to do this and occupies our hands so that they aren't free to love people. One of the dangers is that, sooner or later, when the beach ball comes up, it often surfaces at an angle, with inappropriate behavior and tremendous force.

"If we could go to a counselor or pray together with other people, allowing these unacceptable beach ball-like thoughts or behaviors to begin to come to the surface, our hands would be free to love. The problems are still there, but we are better able to deal with them because now we can see them. When we hold down our unacceptable feelings, tying up our energies, we are psychologically crippling ourselves as Christians. Letting these things surface involves confession, but it is very difficult to confess or be honest unless we feel safe. It's just too threatening. That's when it is vital to have a small, committed group to pray and share with, or a good counselor."

Andrea, too, is an enthusiast of both group therapy and one-on-one counseling. She saw a professional counselor for a year during and after her divorce. She was determined to analyze her part of the problem in her first marriage. She wanted to know where she had manipulated, when she hadn't communicated, or when she had lied to herself. She didn't want to just talk things over with a few friends only to be assured, "It will work itself out." She wanted answers or, at least, possible directions, not platitudes.

During the divorce and in the early months of singleness, she became involved in a church sharing group. Although, of the fourteen members, she was the only unmarried person, she felt comfortable attending and was willing to risk saying a little bit about who she thought she was. No one in the group was allowed to probe or frighten anyone else.

"The group did various exercises designed to develop trust," recalls Andrea. "Since they were optional, I never would do them. I especially remember one in which a person would lie on the floor and the other members would cooperate in lifting him or her toward the ceiling and back down. Everybody except me thought this was wonderful. I would lift, but I would not be lifted."

Looking back, she realizes she was testing to see if the group was really free and the exercises truly optional. Sure enough, no one ever condemned her for refusing to be lifted, saying, "What's wrong with you? Why won't you do it?" Instead, they affirmed her decision with the words: "If you don't want to, that's okay." She was accepted as part of the group even though she chose to limit her participation. Gradually, she learned to trust the members a little more.

"The last night we met was the Wednesday before Christmas. We played a game in which each of us asked the group for a Christmas present. When it was my turn, I asked to be lifted. I had finally reached that point of trust when I was willing to put myself into their care."

The group experience helped Andrea open up and speak honestly about herself to others and also created a way for her to interact with married men and women. Whenever she was around couples, she adopted a false bravado about her single status. She would boast about her no-strings life style, painting only the good side and avoiding the bad. She now believes this attitude only increases the tension that often exists when couples mix with singles in a social setting.

"As a single I was afraid of married people. Often they seemed to be eager to match me up with an appropriate person—so there would be an even number of people at the dinner table, for example. Sometimes I felt much like a friend of mine who aptly said, 'People need partners for some things, but eating isn't one of them.' This same friend once asked, 'What are we doing, lining up for the ark?' I resented the whole 'matchmaking' mentality because I thought it meant that in the eyes of the married couples, I was a lonely, miserable person."

"Therapy and membership in a small group represent only part of one positive way to grow as a single person," says Keith. He suggests the single period be spent completing the unfinished work of adolescence. He urges divorced singles not to remarry for at least a year because of the danger of rebounding, marrying for the wrong reasons, or not allowing sufficient time to work through the grief of the first, unhappy marriage. Andrea is even more conservative—she recommends a waiting period of at least two years.

"In divorce," says Keith, "so many people assume it was the other person's problem. They believe the other guy made the big mistakes so, therefore, they'll just go out and find a nice new mate—maybe a blonde or a brunette this time—without all those hangups. Then, suddenly, the same old issues surface in the new marriage and the realization comes that perhaps the blame for the first failure wasn't so one-sided after all."

Certainly one of the weakest reasons to marry or to remarry is the desire for "legitimate" sex. Christians are taught not to engage in premarital sex, yet they are human with human needs. Whenever they meet someone to whom they are deeply attracted sexually they often think immediately of marriage. Any alternative except abstinence is classified as sin.

"If we deal with this question from a legalistic perspective, there is only one answer: Christians should wait until marriage for sexual intercourse," says Keith. "But, if a person has already gotten into sex before marriage, I believe God can certainly give that person a new chance. Jesus was not legalistic and expressed Himself in ways that lead me to believe He clearly feels rules were made to serve people and guide us into a better way of life."

As to how Jesus would deal with the couple that rushes into marriage prematurely in order to be legalistically correct, Keith admits uncertainty. He wonders if the couple would be marrying out of lust as a primary motivation and if that, too, wouldn't be a sin.

"I would advise people to think and pray long and seriously before getting into a first *or* second marriage. Unless they feel a deep sense of rightness about spending the rest of their lives with a prospective mate, they should wait, both for marriage and for sex. I believe that having legitimate sex and ruining two or more lives in order to keep oneself 'pure' could wind up being a very big sin, even if 'legally' irreproachable."

Again he stresses the importance of intimacy. Sex, he says, turns out to be wonderful when it is mixed with the kind of intimacy that a healthy marriage relationship allows. For that reason he encourages couples to learn all they can about being close and sharing openly with each other before marriage and before sex.

"You can't encourage people by giving them rules. They know the rules already. The thing they're after is not just sex itself, but the experience of intimacy. True intimacy with someone should be like our relationship with God. With it comes confession, forgiveness, acceptance, a new life, a new start."

Although he speaks from his own experience, Keith is the first to admit he doesn't have all the answers. He and Andrea decided a long time ago to trust God to forgive their marital failures and accept their current relationship. There was a time when they wondered if they should adhere strictly to Scripture and grind out their separate lives alone because they could never be "legally" married in the eyes of many church people. But they believe, instead, that God would prefer that they marry and commit their lives and their marriage to Christ and to doing His will.

"I don't *know* that this is right," says Keith. "My own feeling is that I must trust Jesus to forgive and heal a person who has dissolved what had ceased to be marriage in any but a legal sense. I am trusting that, when such a person finds another Christian to love and marry, he will find that Christ's forgiveness is greater even than the law. I have bet my spiritual life that this is true. In remarrying, I bet my life on Jesus Christ in a way I never had before, and that's the bottom line. But I think that's the bottom line with Jesus on everything. It's just that in remarriage, we jump a chasm instead of a creek, in faith. To me that's what it takes."

One thing Keith and Andrea hope that single and married people will understand is that a Christian can lead an absolutely first-class life and remain single always. There is often an implication in some congregations that only if people get married can they really be fulfilling God's will. But of course if that were true, what would they say about Paul . . . and even Jesus?

"When Jesus made the statement about divorce in Matthew 19, it was as if He were reaching up into the moral night, poking stars into the heavens. We can look at those stars and chart our course through life, even though in our humanity we can never reach the perfection of the stars themselves. He taught with those kinds of absolutes, knowing we cannot keep them. If we could we wouldn't need the forgiveness for which we claim He died."

Elisabeth Elliot

*E*lisabeth Elliot is nationally known as a speaker and as the author of fifteen books. The first of her books, Through Gates of Splendor, *is the story of the life and death of her first husband, missionary Jim Elliot, who was killed by members of a South American Indian tribe to whom he was attempting to take the gospel.*

Though she continues to use the name Elisabeth Elliot, under which she has written for the past twenty-five years, she is presently married to Lars Gren, who acts as her manager and agent. They travel together on most of her speaking engagements. She is writer-in-residence at Gordon College, Wenham, Massachusetts, near her home in Magnolia.

Elisabeth Elliot

Till Death Do Us Part

Elisabeth Elliot made a promise to Addison Leitch when he proposed to her.

"There are a lot of things—such as money or good looks—other women could give you that I can't. But one thing I know others can't outdo me on is appreciation. I know how to appreciate what I have in a husband," she recalls saying.

Their marriage, described by Elisabeth in superlatives, was cut short by cancer. After a few brief years of happiness she was returned to the solo ranks, a status she knew inside out. Tragic death had claimed first husband Jim Elliot after just twenty-seven months of marriage. Thirteen years of widowhood had followed.

If firsthand experience is any yardstick of expertise, Elisabeth is an authority on both married and single living. She prefers the former—she's now the wife of Lars Gren—but has twice coped with the latter, after finding herself suddenly single.

"During one of my periods of widowhood I was asked to talk to a group of seminary wives on the problems of being a widow. I refused. I said I'd be glad to talk to the seminary wives, but not on that topic. I didn't regard widowhood as a problem, but as the sphere in which I was to glorify God at that time. When I was single, I was to glorify God as a single; when married, I was to glorify God as a wife; when widowed, I was to glorify God as a widow."

Neither does she think the state of being single is a problem. She admits impatience with people who constantly bemoan the fact they go to bed alone at night, or occasionally eat their meals in solitude, or aren't currently traveling through life in tandem with someone. Accept it, she urges. Stop the endless discussions, definitions, analyses, and tears. She claims that dwelling on marital status is not only immature, but selfish.

"I'm frequently asked how we should handle bitterness and loneliness. We don't *handle* them; they're among the terms of our lives. Every individual is lonely in some way or another. A wife can be just as lonely as a single person—maybe more so in some ways. The question, 'How do you handle loneliness?' implies there's some neat gimmick or trick to solving the feeling of loneliness. I'm sorry, but there isn't. Loneliness must be taken to God; must be borne, endured."

And she has endured loneliness on several occasions. After the death of her first husband she lived alone in the jungle as a missionary for seven years. She had no church for spiritual replenishment, no telephone to share news with family, and no friends to help.

"To follow Christ, we must take up crosses. Part of my cross at that particular time was isolation and loneliness. We pay that price by enduring these things, not by trying to solve them or talking about them or crying about them. Just enduring them."

Endurance. She likes that word. She believes in it. She lives it. The Bible never promises that we will escape suffering, she continues, and God never guaranteed we would be delivered from hurt. But He did guarantee His presence throughout our pain. And that's good enough for Elisabeth. It has seen her through the periods of loss and mourning following her spouses' deaths. It has buoyed her spirits and given her the strength to live a useful life and to be receptive to new happiness.

"The best advice I can give anyone who is going through suffering of any kind is first to accept it, without gritting teeth, or clenching fists, or saying, 'Well, I guess I have to take this because it's the will of God.' Too often people grudgingly say, 'I guess this is my cross. I've got to live with this drunken husband.' Or, 'I've got to be widowed the rest of my life.' Or, 'I've got to put up with this impossible person at work.' Instead, why not say, *Yes, Lord, gladly I will accept this for Your sake?* Offering the suffering back to God is then material for sacrifice."

Living alone for so many years and fulfilling the heavy responsibilities of single parenthood for her daughter confirmed Elisabeth's belief that an individual, if need be, can function alone. Still she stoutly upholds a supportive role for wives. Although she claims to have an assertive personality, she's not ashamed that her view of women is a bit traditional.

"For me, a *bit* traditional would be the understatement of the year. I believe the Scriptures make very plain the roles of men and women. What women should do and what men should do are not merely socially conditioned. They are founded on reality with a capital 'R.' This is how God arranged things. The reason it's traditional is because it's the way God intended it to be."

She urges women to go back to the Bible to find their rightful place in life. Although a sort of tug of war exists between the world and the Scriptures as to woman's role, she sides with the Bible. The fact that God chooses for Himself masculine pronouns underscores her conviction. She believes it's not by accident that in the Old Testament He calls Himself the Bridegroom in relationship to Israel and, in the New Testament, in relationship to the church. She sees the Bridegroom as One who initiates; He is the Wooer who pursues, wins, draws, and loves a person. Love is the aggressor, she claims; femininity, therefore, means response.

She's not alone in her interpretation. Once she asked British theologian Dr. James Packer for his definition of masculinity. His answer? *Acceptance of responsibility.* He cited Adam's responsibility to care for Eve. He reminded her that the word *husband* implies being cared for or cherished.

"There's a great distinction between 'bossism' and authority. The Scriptures don't give a man a warrant to be bossy or overbearing," she says. "He is the head not by achievement, but by assignment. God has assigned him the position. My husband is my head not because he chooses it or earns it or because I prefer it that way. I don't happen to be a retiring, shrinking-violet type. Neither of us has a choice. The husband *is* the head of the wife, as Christ is the Head of the church."

In order for a woman to feel truly feminine, she must be confronted by a thoroughly masculine man, says Elisabeth. She suggests that one seldom thinks about being short until he stands side by side with a very tall person; or about being black or white until he talks with a person of a different color. She sees these as delightful variations of God's creation. Sex is the major differential, and she labels any attempt to erase the distinction between men and women as "demonic."

"I can't emphasize strongly enough the dangers in ignoring the different natures of the sexes. A great many ministers have copped out in this by default without even a thought for the seriousness of the matter. If we think sexuality is unimportant or just a trivial, anatomical distinction, it's no wonder we have a rash of divorces, homosexuality, and women's ordination into the clergy. The differences between men and women involve more than the biological."

Not that she thinks women are destined to make bread or darn hubby's socks for life. As a well-known speaker and author of fifteen books, she's proof positive that a woman can be both supportive at home and successful in the world. She also believes a woman can excel in her work without doing so at the expense of someone else.

"We must be able to distinguish between doing our work for the glory of God and trampling all over everyone in order to get where we want to go because of our worldly ambitions. I've always believed that, to be a writer, I must be willing to be judged by the same standards as all the other writers in the world. I never consider the distinction between men and women. To me, that has absolutely nothing to do with the quality of my writing."

What she writes, of course, comes out of what she is—a white, middle-aged Protestant women who lives in the United States in the twentieth century. She refuses to use her sex or the fact she's a Christian as an excuse for any shortcoming in her work. She expects to be subjected to the same tough standards applied to any other professional author.

"I call a Christian plumber because he is a good plumber," she says, "not because he is a Christian. He doesn't deal with Christian drains or work with Christian tools. The same thing holds true for writers. The world doesn't necessarily want Christian writers. It wants good writers. The awful truth is that I haven't made it into *New Yorker* magazine, not because I'm a Christian, but because I'm not a good enough writer."

A favorite passage from the Bible is Paul's statement that "Whatever you do, do it all for the glory of God" (1 Cor. 10:31 NIV). Because she does not believe in doing a sloppy job for God, she works hard at writing and even harder at being the kind of wife she feels is in keeping with Christian principles. Her advice to married couples is simple: "Wives, submit to your husbands. . . . Husbands, love your wives" (Eph. 5:22, 25 NIV). Although many experts claim communication is the way to a strong marriage, Elisabeth stresses companionableness.

"I don't think a couple must be able to carry out high-powered intellectual conversations, or even be interested in very many of the same things. But each must enjoy the other's company. My second husband was fond of saying that a *very* generous wife may find that her husband lives up to about 80 percent of her expectations. She has a choice: She can pick away at the other 20 percent for the rest of their married life, probably not reducing it by very much, but succeeding in making their lives miserable. Or, she can elect to enjoy the 80 percent."

Elisabeth always tries to enjoy the 80 percent. Because of that, she has had three extremely happy marriages. Each was as different as the circumstances surrounding the courtship. She recalls as a young woman feeling "a veritable hurricane of passions" for Jim Elliot. She says her heart told her, *This is the man,* but God said, *Wait.* And so they did. Each was headed to a different part of the world with a different missionary assignment. After five and a half years of waiting for God's clear direction they married, never dreaming tragedy would separate them twenty-seven months later. It would be thirteen years before she would assume the role of wife again.

"In the case of my second husband, there was just as overwhelming a passion, but there weren't the brakes that God had put on before. We didn't have the red lights, so we got married quite soon, within a few months after we found out we were in love. We had a great marriage because we both had been widowed and, therefore, probably had a higher degree of appreciation for marriage."

And the third, current union?

"In the case of Lars, he pursued me for four years. I knew that I loved him, but it took much prayer and waiting on God before He gave me direction."

Drawn by her candor, people who are considering a second relationship after a happy marriage deluge her with questions. They want to know about the adjustments and difficulties of a second or third marriage.

"I'm always being asked, 'Do you make comparisons among your three husbands?' The answer is 'Why not? Of course I do!' How could I possibly not make comparisons? But the Lord gave me verses which helped to confirm the decision to marry Lars. 'There are different kinds of gifts, but the same Spirit . . . the same God works all of them in all men' (1 Cor. 12:4 NIV). Men do have very different gifts—my husbands have had very few things in common."

Two common traits, however, have been prerequisites to any relationship for Elisabeth. All three of the men in her life have shared them.

"To me, masculinity is at the very top of the list. He's got to be a man who is glad to be a man, without any apologies. Of course, he certainly has to be a Christian."

Each marriage had another common factor—commitment. "When a couple stands up in front of witnesses and Almighty God and says those vows, they are declaring that this is what they *will* do, not what they feel like doing. In sickness, in health, for richer, for poorer, till death do us part. Anybody who goes into marriage with the idea, *Well, I hope this works,* or *We're going to stick together as long as we feel good about each other,* isn't going to be married very long at all."

Tough words, but she believes them. She also believes the church should be very cautious about advising divorced persons to enter into a new marriage. What about the children of each partner? She recognizes the problems of suddenly assuming a ready-made family. Real life is seldom like the madcap harmony of the "Brady Bunch."

Being a single parent is not an impossible burden and certainly should not be the prime motivation for re-marriage. When Elisabeth found herself a young widow with a new baby to rear, she quickly decided not to try to be all things to her daughter, but merely to try to be the best mother she could be. The goal was the same as if her husband had been living.

"People have often asked me, 'How in the world could you be father and mother to Valerie?' The answer is I never tried. I was her mother; I couldn't possibly be her father. She doesn't remember her own father at all, but she had a stepfather through the important years of thirteen to seventeen."

Although Elisabeth adjusted well to her role as single parent and widow, at no time did she doubt that the world she was traveling through as a single is actually geared to couples.

"I was very aware of being a misfit, both when I was single before I married and when I was a widow. A certain amount of anger is expressed by singles who say everybody acts as though everyone is supposed to be married. They complain that the whole world revolves around married people—even the church. It was obvious to me when I was single that God wants most people married. He wants them to have families."

Of course there are exceptions. Singleness is a valid way of serving God, and she cites 1 Corinthians 7 for a list of reasons why Paul thought it was better to be single and why he wished everyone were like him.

"There are many jobs that cannot be done by any-body but singles. As long as I was single there was no question in my mind that this was God's will for me, period! I didn't live my life on tenterhooks thinking, *When am I going to be 'normal'—married, that is?* As a missionary I honestly thought I would be single all my life."

She urges unmarried persons not to wallow in their solo state and not to expect special treatment.

"Let's be graceful about accepting our single place in life and not expect married people to be solicitous and hover over us and surround us and prop us up and do things for us. It's natural for couples to want to get to-gether with other couples. It's very natural for married people to feel a bit off-balance and, perhaps, a bit threatened by having a single person around a lot. I think it's wrong to complain about this."

Instead of focusing too much on the marital issue, singles should go about their lives, making their own contributions by utilizing their own unique talents. God will decide if and when marriage is right for an individual. He did for Elisabeth, even though she tried to put the question completely out of her mind in order to answer what she believed was her calling.

"I struggled with my own willingness to go into the mission field as a single. I decided I would be a missionary even if it meant my chances of marrying would be practically 'zilch.' I didn't want to be single but I came to the place when I said, *Lord, I really believe that your plan for me is joy.* To me, marriage looked like a good thing, but I trusted God enough to believe that if it were a good thing for me, He would not withhold it. But only God knew whether it was good."

Love found her three times, not by chance, but by design—God's design, she believes. Between marriages she continued to strive toward her primary goal, which she says is to glorify God and to do His will. At one point this involved bringing the gospel to the same primitive tribe that had murdered her first husband. At another time it involved writing about her experiences in the jungles of South America. These tasks left little time for concern over her marital status. She left that situation entirely up to God.

"If we really believe that God's ultimate purpose for us is fulfillment, then one of the most crucial areas in which we have to learn to trust Him is in our love life. From all human reasoning it looks as though there cannot possibly be fulfillment without a mate. I just held onto that verse in Psalms that says, 'No good thing will He withhold from them that walk uprightly' (Ps. 84:11)."

Just as many women look to Elisabeth as a role model, so does she have several women who stand as her ideals of true femininity. Interestingly, many are women in their eighties. She marvels at their dignity, serenity, and wisdom. They, like she, have a strong, unshakable sense of their priorities. Often she is asked by younger women—singles and wives—what goals should they set? And how might they better know Jesus?

"I would say, 'Get to know God,' and the clue to getting to know God is: 'If you love me, you will obey what I command. Whoever has my commands and obeys them, I too will love him and show myself to him' (John 14:15, 21 NIV). Obedience is the only route to the knowledge of Christ. This is at the top of the list; no other goal could be higher."

"The best advice I can give anyone who is going through suffering of any kind is first to accept it, without gritting teeth, or clenching fists, or saying, 'Well, I guess I have to take this because it's the will of God.' Instead, why not say, 'Yes, Lord, gladly will I accept this for Your sake'? Offering the suffering back to God is then material for sacrifice."

Charlie and Martha Shedd

Charlie and Martha Shedd are Iowans who graduated from the University of Northern Iowa and Coe College, going on to study at McCormick Presbyterian Seminary and The University of Chicago Divinity School. They have served in pastorates in Colorado, Nebraska, Oklahoma, Texas, and Georgia.

The parents of five and grandparents of four, they are also the authors of twenty-five books, all concerned with marriage and the family. Their newspaper column, "How to Stay in Love," is currently in syndication and they appear on the nationally syndicated television show, "PM Magazine," speaking on the same subject.

They are actively involved in work with The Abundance Foundation, which provides animals, machinery, and buildings for use by the Presbyterian Training Center for retarded teen-agers; and hunger relief efforts in agricultural missions.

Charlie and Martha Shedd
A More Perfect Union

When Charlie and Martha Shedd built their "tree house" on an island twenty miles out in the Atlantic Ocean, the do-it-yourself project was a throwback to pioneer barn-raising days—or, in the Shedds' case, more of a barn-*razing* event.

With the help of a few well-muscled friends, they collapsed a dilapidated mule barn, recycled the wood, and erected in its place a comfortable hideaway in the lofty pines of Fripp Island, offering a panoramic view of the entire East Coast. And the address (no fooling) is Frogmore, South Carolina.

Next on the Shedds' priority list is to enroll in a night class in electrical engineering to learn how to wire the place. Even tree houses need a lamp or two, and while both Charlie and Martha are enthusiastic fans of romantic candlelit dinners, they realize some jobs are better accomplished under a seventy-five-watt bulb—like writing books (they already have twenty-five to their credit); col-

113

laborating on their syndicated newspaper column, 'How To Stay In Love," and a set of films called "The Fun In Marriage Workshop"; and toiling over a difficult jigsaw puzzle to be framed and hung in the tree house.

"We do a lot of studying together," says Charlie. "We think it's important to keep our minds alert to new things. Our hobbies run the gamut from woodworking to rug braiding; bicycling to tennis; swimming to beach walking."

Everything is always done in tandem, of course, a habit established thirty-nine years ago when the young pastor from Iowa took as his bride the pretty coed from the University of Northern Iowa. Their enormously successful ministry is based on their enormously successful marriage. They've built a career upon this happily-ever-after relationship. They counsel couples, conduct "Fun in Marriage" workshops, and even offer tips via regular television appearances on how to keep love alive and lively.

So what's a nice couple like this doing in a book about singles?

"We work with singles a lot," says Martha. "It's amazing how often we're invited to speak at colleges and universities. We've found that the gap between ourselves and young people actually narrowed as we became grandparents. We think there are two reasons the young would listen to the older generation: One is our candor—no topic is *verboten*. Another is our willingness to listen without judging.

"Example? We don't believe in premarital sex or extramarital sex. That's our basic stance. Yet we know that literally thousands of singles with whom we work are into sex. So what will we say: 'You are going to hell, you awful, awful people'? No, our attitude must be: 'We don't believe in what you're doing, but we love you; we care for you, and life styles are something you must settle with the God who made us to glorify Him.'"

Sometimes Charlie's and Martha's contemporary

views cause conservative church leaders—and, occasionally, entire denominations—to shudder. But such criticism, and even ostracism, doesn't discourage the Shedds. *Somebody* has to face sensitive issues with the young. Why shouldn't those *somebodies* be happily married, gray-haired grandparents, turned on by the Bible, and tuned into the times?

"Parts of my book *The Stork Is Dead* practically blew the lid off some denominations. One denomination in particular banned us and our books. Now, several years later, we are being invited by that same denomination to speak often in their churches. I guess our material seems mild in comparison to much which has come out in the meantime."

Disapproval can work both ways. If some churches object to the Shedds' airing of intimate topics, Charlie and Martha take issue with certain groups' unbudgeable conservatism. For example, they believe that a couple's physical relationship is spiritual at its best. They disagree vehemently with the idea that if a person prays enough, his sexual needs will disappear. For them, their recent book, *Celebration in the Bedroom,* supports this argument. In this book they set forth the basic premise that, since sex is spiritual, the more involved two persons become in deep prayer, the more likely they are to become physically stimulated. The Shedds believe it is important for singles to understand this fact.

"We get so upset with religious leaders who tell young people, 'If you were only holy enough, you wouldn't have sex feelings.' That is not true. The holier we are, the more our bodies are turned on in every way. No way could we tell you the number of singles who have said, 'After we started praying together we got so sexually wrought-up that becoming *sexually* involved was an easy next step.' Bible study is another matter and it is an excellent lead-in to marriage.

"In our judgment, not enough couples study the Scriptures together and this has to be one of the major reasons divorce is on the upswing, even among Christian couples.

"We often take surveys of our own and we find that fewer than 5 percent of the Christian couples in America pray together. And fewer than 1 percent study Scripture together in a meaningful way. Why these sad statistics? One reason is the church. The church simply has not trained people to tune in to the Lord together."

Martha says, "I am particularly surprised, even dismayed, when our surveys show that ministers are more lax about studying the Bible in husband-wife relationships than even their lay people. If our test results are correct, the old adage 'Do as I say, not as I do' seems to apply all too well.

"Of course they won't admit it," she adds. "But we conduct our surveys through anonymous questionnaires given at the beginning of our seminars. So there it is, in black and white. Very few of these 'spiritual leaders' are either praying or studying the Scriptures with their families at home."

The Shedd Bible study method is one they've developed through their years together. Individually they read a particular chapter or a book of the Bible. They make notations in the margins. A question mark is penciled in next to the passage which isn't completely understood; a small candle is drawn for new light; and an arrow for conviction. Later, when each has had time to read and reread the biblical selection, they sit down together and discuss their markings.

"It's amazing how this has helped us communicate," says Martha. "Since we explained the system in one of our books, we've heard from other couples who have tried it. Without fail, these study sessions have brought them closer together."

So why this emphasis for singles too? Answer: Good communciation is an absolute must for anyone contemplating marriage relationships. Because it is, the Shedds ask three questions especially for singles.

First: Are you willing to be transparent?

Among the most beautiful words two people can say to each other are: "I want you to *really* know me and I want to *really* know you." But now we come to the basic ingredient for all thorough communciation. This is grace. Nobody is going to reveal himself to another person without assurance that whatever is said will be received with mercy and grace. The spirit has to be, "No matter what you tell me, I am going to love you."

One of the questions most asked of Charlie and Martha is: "Do you think it's necessary for me to tell all my indiscretions?"

"Ideally," says Charlie, "the answer is yes; but in practice, more restraint may be advisable. We urge that any single wishing to unload past guilt on a new partner should be sensitive to his friend's emotions. Can she accept such a confession? Can he weather a detailed account of past involvements and mistakes?

"One of the best letters we've ever received came from a single woman who wrote:

> It was my fault I got a divorce and everyone in our town knew it. I was ashamed. Then Aaron came into my life and wanted to marry me. Finally, one night I simply couldn't stand it anymore. I told him it was time I explained about my past. He said he already knew about it and it didn't matter where I had been. The only thing that was important was where I am now. He said the kind of life I had lived before wasn't anything compared to the kind of life we could have together. We think that's the perfect example of grace—the free unmerited love and favor of God."

Test two for singles contemplating marriage: Is there enough liberty in this relationship? Enough room to grow individually too? Gone are the days when husband made all the rules and wife complied. Charlie and Martha certainly don't endorse any promiscuous, open-marriage concepts. Yet, within the framework of absolute fidelity, spouses must be willing to set each other free in order that each may become the unique self that God intended. This willingness may result in a two-career marriage.

Martha says, "The career woman who gets married, quits her job, and just sits around the house may not make the best wife."

Charlie adds, "But the big problem here is likely to be on the man's side. The average man goes into marriage seeing his woman as someone to minister to his needs, and maybe even to wait on him like mama did. Yet it isn't like that and, in the best two-career marriages we know, the husband not only encourages his wife to live up to her divine uniqueness, but he helps her with the work at home."

The third test for altar-bound singles focuses on the joy of the Lord. *So here's question three: Is this relationship really fun?*

Every couple needs to keep the fun up front. In too many marriages the joy is gone. And why? Maybe they aren't working at the fun side too. People have to work at developing and maintaining a joyous relationship. Fun isn't always automatic; sometimes it has to be planned. Couples need to determine early on whether their fun potential has lifetime possibilities.

Does this mean becoming clone-like in leisure activities? Not for the Shedds. They are living, smiling proof that opposites can establish and nurture happy, lasting relationships.

"When we married we were so opposite the doctor claimed even our blood wasn't compatible. We're inclined to think it's not so much a matter of like *vs.* dislike as it is the ability of one person to view the other as a challenge, a mystery, a wonderful puzzle to put together, and a fun individual to discover. The Bible says 'We know in part' (1 Cor. 13:9). For us the Lord is saying here: 'Now listen, you two, you don't know everything about each other and you probably never will completely, but that's the beauty of it.' Couples marry not because they completely know each other, but because they see so much they want to know about each other. That's why we believe a single should look at a relationship with any future partner as a mysterious, majestic landscape to be discovered, a mountain peak to be climbed, or a stream to be navigated.

"That stream may not always be calm, and that mountain peak might sometimes seem unscalable. Every marriage has moments of friction. The secret is using that friction for even more togetherness.

"We have heard people who say they've never had a fight. Really? Maybe they mean 'We've learned to settle our disagreements without fighting.' We've had some very difficult times in our marriage. There are still moments when we struggle to blend and understand each other. But we've never had a time when we decided to quit. Early on we determined 'We're going to hang in there no matter what.' Yet, we are still in sympathy with couples who have found they can't go on living with dignity in the marriage relationship."

Again, communication has been the Shedds' key to solving their differences.

Charlie says, "I'm very volatile and outgoing while Martha is much more inwardly poised, serene, quiet. I would yell when I got mad, and she'd say, 'I can't take this.' So we made a deal. We agreed to lower our voices one notch when we were angry, instead of raising them two notches, or twenty-two. Of course it was terribly hard, and it still is, to sit down and say very quietly, 'I don't like you and here are the reasons why.' This sharing of hostility also requires a positive base built up through affirmation and praise. Then, when days of hostility come, there is this tremendous affirmative platform to neutralize the hostility. Too often couples pile negative on top of negative on a zero base and that's strictly no good.

"We also believe that flexibility, the ability to change, assures an energy-charged, vital relationship. Stagnation and boredom can breed unhappiness both individually and between partners.

"We have this unusual friend in Miami, an elder in the Presbyterian Church. When he and his wife married, they decided they would put half their income in the bank so that every ten years they could take on an entirely new career. Amazing pair! He's been a carpenter, a realtor, an outdoor guide, and now he's beginning to write!"

Charlie says, "We think this is super and some of our greatest growth periods come from change. When I was pastor in Oklahoma, we built a magnificent new church. So what's next? Next we moved to Houston where we took a salary cut of $4,600 to start a new church. We were so poor. Everyone said we were a bit touched and we even wondered sometimes. But that church grew to 4,000 members. Then from there, we moved to Georgia to a church of sixty-seven people where we would have more time to write."

Such career twists and turns have kept the Shedds enthusiastic about life, about each other, about the plan of God. Yet, over the years, their scenario changes while their relationship remains constant.

It's difficult to imagine Charlie without Martha, or vice versa. But they're candid about the inevitable. Sooner or later one will be returned to the ranks of singleness. They say, "We've discussed this openly with our family, and without getting morbid we should all face facts in every possible way."

The Shedds feel the greatest compliment a spouse can pay a deceased mate is to remarry. To enter into a second permanent relationship is a way of saying that the first marriage experience was so fulfilling and enriching that the widow or widower wants to repeat it.

"We've had a good marriage," says Martha. "Because of that, we're both agreed the one who is left behind after death should remarry."

"Of course," adds Charlie, "it would be a lot easier for her to remarry than me. She is more tuned in than anybody I know. She has a wavelength straight to the heavenly throne. I'm afraid I'd be looking for that kind of wavelength. So I say to her, 'You get married again. I think I'll just hang around the edges for a while.' Our kids' response to that is 'Dad, you'd be married in a week. The dishes would be stacked up, the place would be a mess, and you'd be a basket case in nothing flat.'"

On the subject of parental interference, the Shedds say, "We do a lot of speaking to parents and grandparents and, for the most part this is the approach we recommend they take with their kids: 'Look, I'm ready to tell you what I think whenever you ask me. But until you ask, I'll try to keep my mouth shut.' Now, an amazing thing happens when a parent really gets that idea across. Their kids are more likely to say, 'Hey, mom and dad, what do you think?'"

Since marriage is their field, the Shedds admit their wish is that everyone might one day establish and enjoy a happy, loving, permanent relationship. Yet they are also quick to add, "Even if a first marriage falls short of the happily-ever-after ending, survivors must struggle against the feeling 'I'm a failure, a reject.'"

This feeling can be deadly. It might even lead to defense mechanisms. For instance, the survivors have many single-again friends who say they don't want to be hurt again.

Good question for singles: "Is there any possibility my mind is playing psychological tricks?" So the Shedds urge victims of unhappy relationships to struggle against those bruised and battered, put-down feelings which destroy.

Neither should singles set standards for a mate so high that no one can measure up. Credo: "I must remember I'm not perfect and the person I'm hoping to marry isn't perfect either."

And what of the person who *chooses* to remain single? To these there is only one answer. God is love and if one can experience His love alone, he should be grateful. Only he can know for sure whether he is in God's plan. And if he is, he'll also be wise enough to stay alert for His happy surprises!

"Every marriage has moments of friction. The secret is using that friction for even more togetherness. We've had some very difficult times in our marriage. There are still moments when we struggle to blend and understand each other. But we've never had a time when we decided to quit. Early on we determined 'We're going to hang in there no matter what.'"

Tim Sheppard

*T*he son of a minister, Tim was reared in a healthy Christian environment. He studied classical piano for ten years, received awards for excellence in the National Piano Playing Auditions, and was voted "Most Talented" by his 650-member high school graduating class.

In 1975, Tim won the Amateur Gospel Award of the American Song Festival, over 50,000 entries. He recorded his first album, "Diary," in 1976. Groups such as The Imperials, Truth, Andrus/Blackwood and Company, the Sharrett Brothers, Gary McSpadden, Sound Alliance, and others have recorded his songs. Two albums containing Tim Sheppard songs have won Grammy Awards. He is currently traveling full-time in the United States and Canada, continuing his concert ministry in churches, coffeehouses, colleges, and auditoriums, and has appeared with such well-known artists as Andrae Crouch, Chuck Girard, The Rambos, The Archers, Reba, and Dallas Holm.

Tim Sheppard

Singleminded Living

When singer-songwriter Tim Sheppard began sprouting a few gray hairs at age sixteen, some suggested cure-alls, coverups and Grecian formulas. Just a little dab would do him, they promised, and then the distinguished salt-and-pepper look would be banished forever. Tim listened to their well-meaning advice, but opted to stay natural. He admits his reasons might sound old-fashioned in the cosmetic-conscious 1980s, but he believes if he dyed his hair he would be making the statement that he's not satisfied with how God made him.

His "old-fashioned" ideas don't stop there, but extend to women's clothing, which he pronounces too revealing; current films, which he believes too lust-oriented; and divorce, which he thinks too prevalent.

His views on ladies' apparel:

"A young woman who dresses in a way that causes men to be attracted to her body instead of her countenance would be crazy to expect to be treated like a lady," he says frankly. "I don't like the way some girls dress, so I don't go out with them, knowing somewhere down the line, we'll butt heads on it."

His thoughts on R-rated movies:

"There's no guy on the face of this earth—I don't care how spiritual he is—who can watch a sexually-explicit scene in a film without replaying it in his mind and being tempted by lustful thoughts. Peer pressure adds to the problem. If one member of a group finds the content of a movie offensive and wants to leave, he opens himself up to unbelievable criticism from the rest of the crowd."

On divorce:

"I think divorce is sin, and like any other sin, requires repentance—a turning from that sin to be forgiven. I'm not sure saying 'I know it's wrong to get a divorce, but I'm going to get one anyway' always shows that repentance. And without true repentance, this attitude is a mockery of God's grace. That's my opinion."

At twenty-six, he promotes these basic values during the talk segments of his concerts and in his out-of-the-spotlight life on the road and back at home in Dallas.

"We need to get back to basics," he often tells his audience, "to look at our priorities, and to decide what is superficial in our lives. When I began to try to evaluate how I spend my time, I discovered that it was scary to identify the healthy pastimes and the not-so-healthy ones. Deciding how our time is spent often comes down to discipline—knowing what's right and doing it."

While some performers constantly do battle with inflated egos, Tim carefully tries to fortify himself against self-indulgence by occasionally taking stock of his shortcomings.

"The real secret to keeping our perspective of success in line is having a grip on our Christian identity. I've seen myself, I know what I'm made of, and I don't always like what I see. I know I'm unworthy. I feel sorry for those folks who, by their attitudes, tell others that they've never looked at themselves to find out they are but dust."

Although he might not suffer from the overdose of self-confidence that plagues some entertainers, he shares with them one of the most prevalent hazards of show business—loneliness. He knows many singles struggle with the emptiness of too many hours spent alone, but he claims the loneliness suffered by performers is different.

"People look at a performer differently, and, pretty soon, he may start to believe their evaluation. I have to struggle with the problem of going out with girls who see Tim Sheppard, the singer and songwriter, instead of Tim Sheppard, the person. After an entertainer is pursued for a long time, for all the wrong reasons, he begins to question his self-worth and to wonder, 'Is there anything worthwhile about me besides my music?'"

He used to think of such bouts with loneliness as very negative. A Christian, he thought, should never feel lonely because Jesus is always with him. But now he sees positive aspects of solitude. He believes loneliness can be a magnet at times, drawing him into a deeper relationship with Christ. He admits to being a melancholy person, but often a song comes out of his depression. Loneliness most often strikes him in large crowds, usually after a concert, when he feels he's been misunderstood.

"I suppose it's really unfair to expect people to come up after a concert to compliment me on some deep quality they have detected in my personality. After all, they haven't been exposed to anything more than my stage presence. So they can only comment on my performance."

Still it's the life he has chosen—or, the life that has chosen him. He claims he never intended to be a professional songwriter in the first place. He had studied classical music since he was six years old, played in rock bands in school, and had even written a couple of "My-

Baby-Left-Me" type songs. It was all in good fun until, during his junior year in high school, he made his commitment to Christ.

"Ten years ago, after I accepted the Lord, I started singing around—a song here, a song there—in coffeehouses, churches, and other places. At one point I tried to enter a full-time ministry but all the doors were slammed shut. A temporary warehouse job started to look permanent after a year. I came to a spiritual turning point where I said, *Lord, the doors aren't opening. This really isn't the way I planned it. If You want me to be a shipping clerk, I will; if You want me to be a singer, I will. Just end the confusion and I promise I'll do whatever You want me to do.*"

Within six months his career began its move into high gear. He submitted several songs to the Imperials and one was recorded. He entered an international songwriting competition and was chosen first-place winner over 50,000 entrants in the gospel music division.

"I met Jesus in May of 1971 and began writing Christian songs out of my personal relationship with the Lord. That's how I spend much of my time of prayer and praise—studying the Word and then expressing it through songs. I feel if I ever write songs because so-and-so wants one, or because I can make a certain amount of money, I'll be losing touch with what I need to be doing. A song has honesty and integrity when it comes out of a real experience or out of real praise and worship. I would sacrifice that integrity if I wrote from any other motivation."

His life is now divided into two-week segments—two weeks on the concert circuit and two off. Days at home in Dallas are spent catching up on laundry, correspondence, and telephone calls. Road tours are a string of concert engagements linked by 300-mile stretches between.

"It's a pretty hectic schedule. The concerts each evening are the only real excitement. And, spending a lot of days alone in the van or in hotel rooms causes a real feeling of isolation."

He claims his social life has been virtually nonexistent since he took to the open road several years ago. He doesn't date much when he's on tour because of the risk of being misunderstood. Being considered a "lady's man" certainly wouldn't enhance the seriousness of his ministry, and he wouldn't want to be paraded around as the prize of some celebrity-seeking fan. Too, his old-fashioned values help shape his views on casual dating.

"First of all, is dating strictly a social gig or is it for the purpose of finding a mate? I believe that dating is the first step to finding a permanent partner in life. I don't have the time or the money to date *casually*. As a result, I see dating as a very serious and potentially volatile situation."

He protects himself against emotional involvements that might be harmful to himself or to others by refusing to date non-Christians.

"Scripture advises us not to be unequally yoked (see 2 Cor. 6:14), because wrong companionship can corrupt good morals. The Bible teaches that we should be careful about how and with whom we spend our time."

Even if a young lady can see beyond the stage version of Tim Sheppard, there are still pressures with which to deal.

"A fan's typical image of my wife is someone who looks like Miss America, can sing, and is vivacious and outgoing. All those things don't appeal to me that much. I have no specific requirements for a wife to sing alto and play the piano. I just want to love somebody and have her love me."

In his opinion, marriage is forever. But he cautions that divorce will be common until the sacredness and seriousness of the marriage vows are restored to people's minds. Such vows, made in God's presence, should never be broken.

Before he decides to enter into a permanent partnership with a woman, Tim says he will ask the advice of his parents and friends whose opinions he values. He has suffered from unhappy experiences that resulted when he ignored these sources of help.

"I've gotten involved in disappointing relationships when I ignored my parents' counsel and rushed into something," he recalls. "A lot of marriages today take place without the approval of parents. Setting up a new home by rebelling against two established homes cannot contribute to harmony within the new family."

Any relationship must have a basic foundation of honesty to last a lifetime. There can be pain involved in being truthful, he admits, but there's greater pain in being deceitful.

"A second key to a strong relationship—and this is going to sound strange—is not being too spiritual. No matter how dynamic a man and woman are spiritually, a couple's success will also be determined by their temperaments, likes, dislikes, and compatibility. We need to evaluate relationships on the basis of the chemistry of the involved individuals as well as the spiritual aspect."

While love at first sight might be a cliché, he believes it is possible, although he's never felt it himself. A person who views love as choice and commitment can set his heart in someone's direction and choose to love. A fulfilling relationship doesn't just "happen," though, but should be planned.

"The secular concept of a relationship seems to be, 'Oh, we'll kind of get together and just let whatever happens flow.' I personally believe that a Christian relationship should be directed and goal-oriented. I believe in Proverbs 18:22: 'Whoso findeth a wife findeth a good thing." It doesn't mention a man who casually stumbles into a situation. It implies seeking and finding. If a Christian wants a husband or a wife and doesn't believe he's called to be single, what's wrong with setting out to find someone?"

His pastor once advised him to remain single until his ministry was established. But there are degrees of establishment. Although the number of his fans is growing, his ministry, Servant Outreach, Inc., is still a one-man operation. Tim not only performs on stage, but also writes the music, answers the mail, does the bookkeeping, and mans the phones. He admits to occasionally suffering burnout, when his songwriting ability grinds to a halt and he must wait anxiously for inspiration.

"I usually write one song every four to eight weeks with a dry spell between. Once, after a *real* dry spell, I thought, *I've got to write something,* so I sat down and forced myself to do so. The song seemed meaningless.

"A song usually starts building up inside of me like a storm brewing. I feel a heaviness and know something's going to come out eventually. First comes the chorus (usually), and then the music and lyrics of the verses. I carry a little tape recorder around with me so if I hear a melody or have an idea I can record it and review it later."

Life on the road can also be an ordeal, sometimes causing Tim to question the success of his concert ministry. Vibrations from an audience may vary from one night to the next. Monday's fans might be interested only in being entertained—no messages, please, just music. Tuesday's audience might have a "show-me" attitude— sitting back or standing in judgment. Wednesday's crowd might be downright cold.

"The hardest thing is the issue of acceptance. I feel that probably half the length of the concert is spent in developing rapport with the audience. The Christians are all asking, 'Are you for real? Show us your stuff.' Any singer can *sing* all night, but sooner or later I have to *talk,* and that makes or breaks me as far as my credibility goes. Sometimes it's so painful I want to say, 'Hey, why waste my time and yours? I'll refund your money. I'd rather be with my family.'

"I'd enjoy singing much more if I had instant rapport when I first walk out on the stage. That's happened to me on a few occasions, and when it does, I know the people are on my side, they believe in me, they're pulling for me, so I just close my eyes and sing my heart out."

He's still experimenting with concert formats. Sometimes he opens by singing so many songs the audience begins to wonder if he's ever going to speak. But he wants to be sensitive to the mood of the fans and know when they are ready to hear a spoken message.

Other evenings he jokes with the audience about how people are enthusiastic spectators at sports events but hesitate to get actively involved in church services and Christian concerts.

"I try to turn it around so the people discover they can be ministered to and enjoy themselves at the same time. Of course, sometimes after twenty minutes I feel like saying, 'You don't want to be here; I don't want to be here; let's go home.'"

If the fans are receptive, they find his message palatable and easily digested. He stresses the close relationship between God and man, and refutes the idea that people are not valuable to the kingdom of God.

"We have a school of thought that says that God, in the beginning, was lonely and needed fellowship and companionship. This is how we like to talk about singles today. We are valuable, not because God needs us, but because He loves us. The greatest reason to love is to love for no reason at all."

Just as God created the heavens and earth out of nothing, so did He bring spiritual life to us out of waste and void, says Tim. He preaches that God can bring strength out of weakness. If we are strong Christians today, it is because Christ is in us. This link, which he calls the relationship between humanity and divinity, is a favorite subject to discuss with audiences.

"Too many times in Christianity we've tried to sever our humanity from the divinity of God. We say, 'Okay, I'm a Christian now. I'm never going to be depressed; I've got all this power and strength and I'm going to go out and slay the Devil by myself and set the world on fire for God.'"

He urges people to look at Jesus' life and realize that what has appealed to Christians over the years is the fact God is *in* man, not segregated *from* man. Everyone is familiar with the miracle in the Bible when Jesus turned water into wine at the marriage at Cana. To Tim, the significance of the story was not in the miracle of the wine, but rather in the fact that Jesus cared enough about human life to even attend the wedding and mingle with the guests.

"Not only is it beautiful that Jesus could heal broken hearts, but that He could be broken for us. Not only is it beautiful that He worked miracles, but that He required sleep. Somehow, in Jesus, humanity and divinity came together. Humanity apart from divinity has no hope, but divinity apart from humanity has no expression."

He believes that man comes closest to God's love when he establishes a permanent relationship with a mate. This special kind of relationship calls for each partner to share the most intimate of thoughts, and to know the other's faults and problems, yet love each other without question or doubt. He hopes to enjoy such a relationship someday, although he realizes meeting the right person and nurturing such a friendship isn't always easy with his topsy-turvy schedule. Tim has tried singles' church groups and has mixed feelings about their programs and purposes.

"If singles are only exposed to other singles, they never have good examples of biblical marriages. I feel the same way about the elderly. While there should be a ministry for senior citizens, they shouldn't be isolated from the mainstream. I've been involved in a couple of situations in singles' ministries in which I felt the emphasis was too much on matchmaking. I don't think we should treat singles or any other group as unique breeds to be handled with special care. There's a danger of imbalance."

He warns other singles that marriage is not some ideal state that will solve all difficulties. In some ways it can cause new complications as two lives blend into one. He knows his own life style, certainly in respect to travel, would become more difficult if he were half of a Mr. and Mrs. duo. But still, the joy of having someone close would be a comfort to him.

"Marriage can be very complicated or it can be a real blessing. I know too many people who decide what will make them happy and build their plans around it, never consulting the Lord. When the Lord readjusts their plans they object, saying, 'I'm not going to like this; I'm not going to feel secure.' It should be the reverse. The key is trusting the Lord with our future, with all our hearts, and then acknowledging Him in all our ways and letting Him direct our paths (see Prov. 3:6). We're not obligated to tell God what to do. We're obligated to trust Him to lead us."

A single person shouldn't assume that he will marry. Nor should his happiness hinge on his perception of the future, says Tim. He particularly objects to the idea of earmarking certain prerequisites to happiness and then praying that God will bless the plan.

"We are guilty of setting goals for ourselves and then saying, *Okay, God, give me the strength to reach my goals.* God then becomes the means to an end, whereas God Himself should be the end."

Tim decided way back in high school to trust the Lord on matters of his career—shipping clerk or singer?; his heart—single or married?; and even his head—gray hair and all.

"I believe that dating is the first step to finding a permanent partner in life. I don't have the time or the money to date casually. As a result, I see dating as a very serious and potentially volatile situation. Scripture advises us not to be unequally yoked, because wrong companionship can corrupt good morals. The Bible teaches that we should be careful about how and with whom we spend our time."

Jim Smoke

*J*im *Smoke spent several years as pastor and Youth for Christ director. While serving as Senior Minister to Single Adults at Robert Schuller's Garden Grove Community Church, he developed one of the world's largest and finest singles' ministries, and during this time, with his staff, began publication of* Solo *magazine. He is currently serving on the staff of the First Presbyterian Church, Hollywood, California. Smoke continues to be in great demand as a speaker and is the author of* Growing Through Divorce.

Jim Smoke

Singular Minister

In some ways Jim Smoke is an unlikely candidate for the title of America's foremost authority on singles' ministries. After all, he's happily married, and he and his wife Carol have three teen-agers. But requiring a singles' minister to be single is like saying a marriage counselor must be married or a heart surgeon must suffer palpitations.

Smoke knows the singles' scene inside out. He began directing the enormously successful Single Adult Ministries at Robert Schuller's Garden Grove Community Church in California and now criss-crosses the country as a guest speaker and workshop leader for singles' groups. He's adaptable—as willing to swap ideas with a fledgling singles' fellowship over hamburgers and fries as to address a standing-room-only banquet for urban church leaders. The days on the road may be numbered, however, since he misses the laboratory atmosphere of running a singles' program. His homing instinct is strong and he likes being tied to a ministerial base.

"I can't feel comfortable trying to share verbally things with which I'm not experimenting," he explains. "I want to be able to try things and see them work or fail. Then I can honestly say, 'We've tried it; it's a good idea ... it works.' I also miss the supportive community of staff members. I like coming home from a road trip and being asked, 'How'd it go?' They share in my ministry and provide constant prayer support."

He sees singles' ministries today as being at the same growth stage as youth ministries were in the 1950s (from which "Youth for Christ" was born). A need has been recognized among the exploding single adult population, and the needs are varied: single parenting, divorce, rejection, loneliness, isolation, etc.

"For so long, singles in the church have been colored a sort of gray. Now the church is slowly waking up and saying, 'Hey, here's a group of people whose needs are as important as anyone else's.' I'm not saying a singles' ministry is *the* ministry to be reckoned with, but it's as valid as any others in the church and it demands and deserves attention, budgeting, and staffing."

The secular world learned this years ago and started vying for singles' time and money, claims Smoke. Recreation centers sponsored "get-acquainted" nights, singles' bars cropped up, and special vacation tours and cruises were advertised "For Singles Only." Smoke thinks it's important for churches to offer another option to people who want the fellowship and support of other solos without compromising their beliefs or lowering their standards.

"A church-sponsored singles' ministry is an alternative to some of the secular single scenes often referred to as 'the meat market' or the 'snatch and grab society.' Here's an opportunity for fellowship without that kind of climate. Here's a place to build friendships in a warm environment. We could almost call it a supportive cocoon type of environment."

A favorite bit of Scripture that Jim Smoke feels applies particularly well to the Christian single is: "I can do all things through Christ which strengtheneth me" (Phil. 4:13). He believes the Christian has a head start on happiness. Of the more than fifty-five million singles in America, those who are Christian can view their struggles with the knowledge that they have an Ally, and that they'll get by with a *lot* of help from this Friend.

"The Christian single can say, 'I struggle with problems like everyone else. The difference is that God equips me to go through the problems and challenges—not around them, not over them, but through them.' He has the ability to say, 'With God's help, I can face loneliness and rejection; I can work through my guilt; I can find answers. The Word of God can become a reality in my life.'"

How do you start a singles' ministry? Slowly, counsels Smoke. As enthusiastic as he is about the growing number of programs geared to Christian singles, he's aware of the problems, too. He knows that to be successful, such a ministry must have the support not only of the group's members but also of the church hierarchy. The pastor. The deacons. The Christian Education Committee. The elders.

"It has to start from the top. The minister in the pulpit must offer the same degree of love and concern to the singles as is given to the junior high group, the senior highs, collegians, married couples, the golden-agers club ... all the other units of the church. There has to be a sense of affirmation. The singles must be acknowledged as a part of the body and the church leadership must share with them as they share with anyone else. Too often singles are treated as an odd unit with unique problems. Singles should feel they are accepted and encouraged to take part in the total life of the church."

Sometimes convincing a church to sponsor a singles' ministry requires a bit of salesmanship, says Smoke. He urges singles to study their church and determine the power structure in order to know which person or group has to be "sold" on the idea. Then it's full speed ahead. If the minister is the key decision-maker, he is the logical person on whom to concentrate these efforts. If members of the board of elders hold the power and the purse-strings, the argument and need presentation must be targeted toward them.

"Many ministers wouldn't touch a singles' ministry with a ten-foot pole because they don't want to deal with the divorce issue. With that kind of resistance, it's extremely difficult to initiate a successful ministry. If you find yourself in a situation where you cannot sell a ministry to the church, you have two options: You either conduct the ministry in a closet—and if you do that, it will probably always *stay* in the closet—or you take it someplace else."

Even the blessing of the church staff doesn't assure success, claims Smoke. But it's a beginning. The next hurdle is the recruitment of strong, dedicated leadership for the group. More dilemmas: Should the program's leader be male or female? Single or married? Young or not-so-young? How long should he/she serve? What kind of training is necessary?

"First, I think it's important to remember that often men won't participate in a program run entirely by women. Men are needed in some areas of leadership. Why? Men are more likely to attract both men and women, while women in leadership tend to attract only other women. To me it's a sociological thing. Also, divorced women, suddenly without male leadership in their home, find they may occasionally need a man's point of view. That's why so many women say to me, 'How can I find a man just to be a friend—someone to talk to? I don't want to marry him or chase him. I only want to be able to have a cup of coffee with him and say, 'Boy, do I need to talk with you about some problems and struggles!'"

Unfortunately, men are scarce in group situations and often don't relate to "clubs" as readily as women do. While women seem to be comfortable as a part of a fellowship experience, men tend to gravitate toward more macho group activities like sports. Then there's the factor of the male ego.

If he's hurting, a man will usually suffer alone rather than turn to a group for help. Society dictates that man is supposed to be in charge of his own life and be able to resolve his own problems. He may feel that he's not *supposed* to need help from somebody else.

As director of the singles' program at Garden Grove Community Church, Smoke recruited leaders from professional ranks—lawyers, bank executives, and teachers. If a member of the singles' group expressed an interest in taking over duties as president or vice president of the organization, Smoke pulled no punches in spelling out all the responsibilities attached to the job. A leadership role carried an obligation of at least ten to twenty hours a week.

"Most people would cry, 'Twenty hours a week!' And then I'd explain, 'Hey, if you do it right, that's what it's going to cost you.' Those demands raised our level of leadership. Once they were involved, the leader believed in what we were doing and became committed. Sometimes they were running classes of up to 200 members."

According to Smoke's plan, no one was expected to hold an office longer than six months. "I don't think many single adults are in a position to make long-range commitments to a program that locks them in. Singles are in transition—they move on to a better job, or get involved in a relationship leading to marriage. Naturally, when that happens, their priorities and commitments change."

On the average, a single is usually involved in a singles' ministry for only about twelve months, especially in more urban areas. Smoke estimates that only 20 percent of the persons who visit a group will stay. The other 80 percent are merely "passing through." Name tags are essential—otherwise how can the leader keep up with who's who? Besides, claims Smoke, if a group doesn't need name tags, chances are it's not growing like it should.

"Single people, for all kinds of reasons, drift in and out of singles' programs. They are in search of relationships—all levels of relationships, not just marital. If I were a guy, forty-two years old, who had lost my wife by divorce or death, I wouldn't settle down in the first singles' group I found. I'd visit five or ten groups in town and ultimately choose one that made me feel most comfortable."

Such "shopping around" shouldn't be limited to men, says Smoke. Women, too, should take the initiative in actively looking for Christian companionship. Gone are the days when demurring ladies sat on the sidelines, playing the passive role.

"Women limit themselves by thinking they must sit home and wait until they're asked out. I don't think it has to be that way. There's really nothing wrong with a woman's openly seeking a significant relationship."

The only problem with such sampling of first one fellowship and then another is that the leadership has difficulty ministering to the "short-term member." How can groups reach out to newcomers if sporadic attendance prevents the relationship from deepening beyond the superficial nametag level?

"We find that quality in-depth time is spent with only 20 percent of the people. With the other 80 percent there is a different ministry. The leaders must touch them lightly, share with them, and bless them, before they're out the door and moving on. This is why a singles' ministry is different from any other. Married people are usually locked in by job or family commitments. Single people are more flexible."

However brief the member's stay, it should be of value. Smoke recommends a program format that is both biblical and relational. The three elements that Jim recommends in a singles' ministry are Bible study on Sunday morning, small group gatherings on Tuesday nights, and occasional socials on weekends or evenings. This three-pronged attack addresses the mental, the social, and the spiritual.

"When I was a kid we used to have roller-skating parties, and right in the middle of skating, everyone would be asked to plop down on the floor and listen to someone preach for twenty-five minutes. It was as if we had to justify having fun by sandwiching in a little Bible study. What a con job! If someone brought a friend who didn't realize he was going to be preached to, many times he wouldn't come back again.

"I don't see Jesus operating that way. He was always sincere and direct. That's why it's important to say to your singles, 'This is fun time so let's have fun,' or 'This is study time when we dig into the Word. If you're serious about growth, come along.' Instead of preaching the Bible at every gathering, we should make sure the visitor is received warmly by the group. That's where I first see changes in people—after they've been accepted and received socially. Only after that do they begin to long for depth in the Word."

Because members and leaders of singles' groups tend to come and go frequently, some kind of continuity is essential. Smoke believes the sponsoring church should designate someone to oversee the program on a long-term basis. The person needn't be an ordained minister, but should be a church staff member or active lay person who is totally committed to the validity and purpose of the singles' ministry.

"I think the person selected ought to have the same kind of qualifications that would be required for Christian education or any other department in the church. He should have the gift of teaching in order to instruct singles in the classroom setting. He should be able to counsel one on one. Sensitivity and the ability to be non-judgmental are two other extremely critical characteristics. If the person hasn't been called by God into the ministry, he's probably just an opportunist. If that's the case, his ministry will fade away."

Whether a single adult or a married couple is most effective at the helm of a certain singles' program is another consideration. The unmarried leader risks being a prime candidate for group members to pursue romantically, but, on the other hand, knows firsthand the struggles of living alone.

Whatever the decision, the designated singles' minister should be a skilled professional who commands and deserves an adequate salary. Too often churches don't take their singles' programs seriously and initiate them more as a fad than a commitment. It's the bandwagon syndrome—"Everyone else has a singles' ministry, so we better start one too." Smoke cringes at such shallow attitudes and issues terse warnings.

"This is serious business. We can't play with people's lives. We need leaders who are trained, skilled, and equipped for working with single adults—people who understand the complexities of today's singles. A lay person can handle it for a while, but over the long haul he wouldn't have the clout. Without some type of full-time leadership, the ministry will eventually flounder or die."

The whole complexion of the singles' group is determined by its staff leaders, says Smoke. It's a case of follow the leader with the leader's setting the pace and acting as role model as well. If he reaches out to others, group members will do the same. It's also the leader's job to integrate singles into the mainstream of church life.

"A singles' ministry runs the risk of becoming an entity within itself—a self-contained unit where the singles do everything with one another and are set apart from the rest of the church body. Although I think they have to have a time when their unique and special needs are met, they also have to have a time of integration with the total church program."

One responsibility *not* included in the job description of a singles' ministry is matchmaking. In fact, Smoke claims the director of a singles' program is more often called upon to slow down a budding relationship by urging the two parties to examine their needs and motives.

"Some people won't admit their needs, and others don't even know what their needs are. However, I've found that people who are becoming whole and are growing are more open to talking about it. They have a freedom to share that's refreshing."

His primary concern about divorce is not that it's a sin—after all, God forgives sin—but the fact that divorced people often repeat their marital mistakes. Too often singles rush into a second "permanent" relationship that again proves to be temporary.

"One of the big problems many churches have is that divorced people bump into each other, develop a quick relationship, and get married. You'd be surprised how quickly some people remarry. The sad thing is that the singles' minister will often have them back in his group within a year. They don't make it; the union fails. There is a desperate need for people to be better equipped for a remarriage situation ... better equipped to handle the issues and unique challenges of remarriage. I say to the divorced contemplating remarriage:

Give yourself time to grow and decide where you are. Don't marry on the rebound. Don't marry out of hurt. Don't marry out of revenge or anguish. A lot of people do. Their hurt is deep, and they are looking for someone to alleviate the pain. Time and growth are two terribly vital ingredients in a healthy marriage."

If a second relationship is strong and well-founded, a different kind of counseling could be necessary. A singles' minister may be called on to dispel any feelings of guilt the couple might have about remarriage. Smoke recalls the case of a divorced woman who said she thought the church had ruled out her option to remarry. She felt locked in a box by a denomination that didn't recognize divorce and therefore was saying to her, "You've sinned and you're going to have to pay for it the rest of your life." Smoke doesn't agree with such a narrow interpretation of God's Word.

"That isn't consistent with my understanding of the Bible's teaching on forgiveness. I believe divorce is a sin and I also believe God forgives sin. Look at John 1:9: 'If we confess our sins, he is faithful and just to forgive our sins, and to cleanse us from all unrighteousness.' It applies to divorced people as well. God isn't saying, 'If you confess your sins, I will forgive all of them except divorce.' Neither do I see God saying, 'I'll forgive you, *but* here's the penalty you've got to live with.' That's not what God's grace is all about. God's over-arching message from Matthew to Revelation is the rainbow of love. In that love is forgiveness. God's love includes full and complete forgiveness for all confessed sin. His grace is beyond our comprehension."

To any church considering a singles' program, Smoke suggests careful planning and a full investigation of the cost, in terms of leadership, dollars, and sense.

"Too many churches are jumping into a singles' ministry before they're ready. They're not asking, 'What kind of leadership produces the healthiest single adult program? How is this going to affect us budgetwise?' They have no plan, and as a result, they get programs like mushrooms—they grow up overnight and then just blow away with the wind. A church must decide what it's willing to pay and at what point it will hire a full-time staffer to shepherd the program."

His advice to singles who might participate in the ministry is equally serious. And, he stresses, his guidelines are just as appropriate for couples as they are for solos.

"I think one of the most important things an adult can remember is to accept circumstances that can't be changed and grow through them. Paul was a good example. Remember when he was in prison? He didn't plan to be there. He didn't like it there. It was painful and unpleasant. Yet his attitude was one of praise. He turned a negative experience into a very positive one. He grew with it. This isn't an issue only for singles. Regardless of our status, we have to accept ourselves where we are, with our limitations. That means stretching and struggling to grow. Just as it takes tremendous pressure to form diamonds, we can allow God to use our circumstances—difficult and stressful as they might be—to refine us into something strong and beautiful."

"For so long, singles in the church have been colored a sort of gray. Now the church is slowly waking up and saying, 'Hey, here's a group of people whose needs are as important as anyone else's.' I'm not saying a singles' ministry is the ministry to be reckoned with, but it's as valid as any others in the church and it demands and deserves attention, budgeting, and staffing."

Richard Dobbins

*R*ichard D. Dobbins, ordained minister and clinical psychologist, served twenty-six years as pastor of Evangel Temple, Akron, Ohio, during which he founded EMERGE Ministries, Inc. He resigned the pastorate in 1976 to become full-time director of EMERGE, a learning resource center dedicated to the development and application of an integration of faith and science to the mental health of Christians.

Dr. Dobbins received his doctorate in Guidance and Counseling from the University of Akron in 1970. He is Assistant Superintendent of the Ohio District of the Assemblies of God and member of the National Board of Education for that church. A former faculty member of the University of Akron and Central Bible College, Springfield, Missouri, Dr. Dobbins is currently on the faculty of Ashland Theological Seminary. He is a frequent Staley Foundation lecturer on college campuses.

Richard Dobbins

Happiness Is . . .

For Dr. Richard Dobbins, "getting away from it all" usually involves no more than ducking into his den for a few minutes and gazing up at a forty-inch muskie mounted on his wall of fame. The fish, according to Dr. Dobbins, represents ten or fifteen minutes of good fun. Sometimes, reliving those moments through fantasy is the only "vacation" he can squeeze into his day.

Dr. Dobbins wears the hat of an angler rarely, but the shoes of the Fisherman daily. He's an ordained minister and licensed psychologist who is closing the gap between the science of psychology and the impact of faith. His approach to this ministry had its roots in personal tragedy. A high school and Bible college dropout, he left the classroom because he believed Christ was returning so soon that he had to prepare the way by preaching the gospel. At nineteen, he and his pretty bride packed their belongings to begin traveling the rural church circuit, ministering to backwoods areas.

But trouble came to the young couple after the birth of their first child. Mrs. Dobbins suffered severe post-partum depression and for many months was despondent and overwhelmed by frustration. The Reverend Dobbins suddenly was faced with a problem he couldn't understand.

"I knew my wife loved God and was very responsible in her devotional life," he recalls. "But here was something apart from her spiritual life with which she couldn't cope. In those days, I couldn't talk with fellow ministers because they often equated emotional problems with spiritual shortcomings. And secular psychiatry tended to attack a person's faith. What could we do? We felt we had no place to go for both spiritual support and psychological insight."

Forced to leave the evangelistic field, they decided to settle in Akron, Ohio, and start a small church. Again, the Reverend Dobbins encountered emotional problems; this time, the ones plaguing believers within his congregation. Determined to help somehow, he visited the nearby University of Akron to see if he could take one or two special classes in psychology. Unaware of his academic potential, he was surprised when he easily passed the entrance exam and was admitted to college.

His original goal of taking "one or two classes" expanded until he had added three impressive "trophies" to that wall of fame in his den—a bachelor of arts and a master of arts in psychology, plus a doctorate in guidance and counseling. Today, Dr. Dobbins is a licensed psychologist and is considered one of the area's finest Christian counselors.

Mrs. Dobbins, now completely healed, is a vibrant part of his work. Of the hundreds of persons he has counseled over the years, some 25 percent are singles —divorced, never-married, or widowed solos. Their ages and marital backgrounds may vary but their goals are similar. They want to find happiness. Doesn't everyone?

Happiness is . . . different things to different people, admits Dr. Dobbins. On the surface it might merely be a good job or a new car—or reeling in the muskie that didn't get away. On a more serious level it might mean maintaining a happy marriage, or, for many singles, meeting someone special and together building a relationship strong enough to last a lifetime. Sometimes counseling is needed to point the way to happiness.

"Singles most often come for treatment during the first few months following divorce," says Dr. Dobbins. "Sometimes they're drowning in guilt because they are into some kind of sexual misbehavior. Often they have questions about managing children in a single-parent home, feeling guilty because they have deprived the kids of a mother or father. Occasionally financial worries cause tension. And, of course, dealing with loneliness and coping with the possibility of a second marriage can present problems."

His advice to singles who are about to enter a new relationship can be summed up in three words: *Take it easy!* He believes every romantic involvement needs several months to blossom and must pass through four stages, beginning with simple *rapport.*

• After two or three dates the single should ask himself, *Can I feel close to this person? Do we hit it off?* If the answer is no, chances are the relationship has little hope of deepening beyond the level of a superficial acquaintance.

• Dr. Dobbins refers to the second step as mutual *self-revelation* and it is at this point most singles— especially women—are hurt. They have a tendency to reveal too much of themselves psychologically—and perhaps physically. When her partner doesn't reciprocate, the woman feels exposed and over-committed.

"If the other person isn't willing to make an equal

psychological and spiritual investment in the relationship, a single needs to see that for what it is and back out," he advises.

- But, if at this point, all systems are still "go," the friendship progresses to phase three, which Dobbins calls *mutual dependency.* It is here that singles can relax, begin to feel really comfortable with each other, call, write, and communicate more often and more openly.

- With the relationship still intact, it's on to stage four—*mutual need fulfillment.*

"This is when each person meets the needs of the other. One is tuned into the other's feelings and knows when to shore up morale, when to offer advice, when to sit quietly and just listen. The rapport tightens, the couple depends on each other, opens up, and shares more and more of themselves."

But Dr. Dobbins warns that there is a prerequisite to such a happy man-woman relationship. A foundation must be built long before introductions are made or the invitation to a first date is nervously extended and uncertainly accepted.

"Happiness and satisfaction in life first have to come out of a relationship with God and with ourselves. The single adults with whom I deal are most likely to get into trouble when they seek from others what can only be obtained through healthy relationships with God and with themselves. I urge my single patients not to depend upon others for their happiness and self-esteem.

"That holds for married couples too. In my own case, I believe I'm sufficiently responsible for my own happiness, regardless of what happens to my wife. She enhances my happiness. Without her I would find it more difficult to be happy, but I don't *depend* on her to make me a happy person. That's up to me."

Before singles can attract the love of others, they must see themselves as lovable, says Dr. Dobbins. They must realize God loves all of us regardless of what we do. This was proven on Calvary.

"We can't do anything to make Him love us more, and we can't do anything to make Him love us less. When we accept this fact, we begin to understand God's love for us as something apart from His pleasure or displeasure with our behavior. We are lovable in God's eyes not because of what we do but because of who we are. We are also valuable. This was demonstrated by the price He was willing to pay for our redemption. And we are forgivable. As far as God is concerned, there is nothing we will ever do, are doing, or have done that cannot be forgiven. Knowing this, we can set aside any excess baggage from the past and get on with the business of living."

Part of the baggage may be the guilt of having gotten a divorce in the first place. Or, for some singles it is the guilt they feel when they realize they want to marry a second time. Is divorce wrong? Is the penalty for divorce a celibate single life forever? Some churches say yes.

"The theological and spiritual issues of divorce are individual matters that have to be wrestled out between the persons who are divorced, their churches (if they are church members), and God," says Dr. Dobbins. He frankly admits he can't condone divorce as an option for two believers experiencing marital conflict. "But once divorce occurs, it seems totally unrealistic to expect the individual to remain single for the rest of his life. Although a divorce may not be biblically justified, neither is it an unpardonable sin. When Jesus sat with the woman at the well, He didn't find her past marital history a hindrance to giving her living water. He didn't tell her with which of her husbands she had to live in order to get to heaven" (see John 4:6–29).

It is a mistake, believes Dr. Dobbins, to assume that divorced persons are a negative influence on married couples. Only a very sick divorced person would deliberately set out to break up happy unions.

"Most people who have experienced broken marriages know the horrible pain that's involved. They are among those who most hate divorce. Assuming they will lobby to encourage other couples to split up is a mistake. While the church should be compassionate toward the divorced, the divorced themselves should be among the believers who encourage a more redemptive solution to a marriage conflict."

Occasionally the issues of divorce and remarriage can put the church in a delicate position. Dr. Dobbins found, in his denomination, a double standard. Persons who had divorced and remarried were "punished" by being refused the right to hold elected church positions. Fine Christians who had led otherwise exemplary lives, these persons had ended marriages because of serious problems such as alcoholism or promiscuity on the part of their partners. Eventually they had remarried in the church and continued as active members, although they were never again permitted to hold a church office.

"At the same time, our church was receiving people from the Jesus movement and the drug culture, some of whom had lived with several sexual partners. Many of them came into our fold, married our sons and daughters, and were allowed to hold elected church positions. So, without really intending to do so, we were rewarding sexual irresponsibility and punishing sexual responsibility. That's the ridiculous position in which many churches still find themselves."

No marriage should be entered into with the attitude: "If this doesn't work we can always get a divorce." An ounce or two of prevention might be the best way to assure a till-death-do-us-part relationship. First, advises Dr. Dobbins, every single with marriage on his mind should take a long look at his future mate's history.

"Women, especially, can be overly optimistic about how the magic of romance will make great changes in a prospective spouse. Actually, the patterns of human behavior become fairly fixed. The social expression of behavior might change but a person's basic personality patterns are not likely to change just because he gets married. By the time an individual enters his mid-to-late twenties, personality patterns are usually well established."

Dr. Dobbins recommends a leisurely engagement period. But not *too* leisurely.

"Studies indicate that engagement periods lasting less than six months or more than two years are not healthy. Somewhere in that time period, a normal adult should be able to decide whether or not to commit to marriage. If after two years a person is unable to make a commitment, I advise the partner to back out rather than invest five, six, or seven years in a relationship that is going nowhere."

Complications may surface during the dating period if one of the singles formerly has been married and has children to consider. According to Dr. Dobbins, some adults can restore equilibrium to their lives in as little as six months after a divorce, but children often require far longer.

"A pre-verbal child will, in many cases, require three years to overcome the trauma of divorce. He might regress to wetting the bed or throwing toys or staging temper tantrums. The elementary school-age child may experience some withdrawal and depression. He might sit and stare out into space. School grades may suffer for a while."

For the single Christian man anticipating marriage to a woman with children, Dr. Dobbins has special words of advice. The man must be secure enough in his own identity to know that, in time, he will come first in the mate's affections. But for the first several months of marriage her children may be closer to her than he is. If that fact bothers him, he should reconsider his decision to take on the new family.

"Children have a way of loving boyfriends and despising stepfathers. Mom's boyfriend is a great person, but when he marries her and moves into the home to compete for family space and her affection, then the children don't give up very easily."

The children may start to misbehave, hammering a wedge between the couple, says Dr. Dobbins. The husband may be tempted to say to the wife, "You're spoiling these children. You should be more firm with them." Neither the mother nor the children welcome this kind of judgment from the newcomer in the family. The mother reaches out to protect her children and they cling to her, thus convincing the new husband he was right after all—the mother *is* too permissive.

"He attacks her management of the children, bringing her to defend them more, in turn driving them closer to her. Before long, mother and offspring are one unit and the new husband is by himself, separate from them."

The situation isn't nearly as hopeless as it may seem, assures Dobbins. The second husband should never try to replace the children's natural father. He should settle for the role of good friend until the time the youngsters make it evident they are ready for a deeper relationship. And he should leave primary discipline to the mother, at least in the beginning. Above all, he should be patient and understanding of all the emotions and fears endured by his new wife and her children.

"This woman has been to the altar once before with a man who promised he'd stay with her till death—but he didn't. She knows she's going to be her children's mother as long as she lives. She's not quite sure—although she's hopeful—that she'll be the second man's wife that long."

Even more difficult is the dilemma of a single woman marrying a man who brings a ready-made family to the union. This problem may become more prevalent as increasing numbers of fathers win custody of their children.

"What we have found is that women usually have more difficulty dealing with the man's children than a man does coping with a woman's children. Often it is very, very hard for a second wife to tolerate her husband's children from a former marriage."

Certainly one old wives' tale which Dr. Dobbins would like to dispel is the belief that all children will suffer unless they have two parents living together at home. If a marriage fails, the parent who has primary care of the children shouldn't feel obligated to go shopping for a spouse to fill out the traditional family unit. A single-parent household can be a happy and successful one, especially if the mother or father doesn't try to accomplish the impossible feat of being both mom *and* dad to the children.

"Single parents often take on themselves too heavy a guilt trip for depriving their children of a second parent. Many, if not most, of the parental problems they face are the same they would have faced had they never divorced. Putting themselves under expectations they can't possibly fulfill can create a cloud of guilt under which the entire family suffers."

Dr. Dobbins suggests that women who are bringing up children alone should arrange for them to spend time with men in the family and church. Uncles, grandfathers, friends, and neighbors can act as role models and even substitutes for the father. Also, Dobbins urges the mother to cultivate an ongoing coparental relationship with the child's natural father. Sometimes this calls for a certain "bigness" on the part of the single parent, but if the father provides support for the child he should have liberal visitation rights.

"It's usually easier for single parents to manage children of their own sex," says Dr. Dobbins. "A boy is usually more secure with his mother until he goes through puberty; then, if the father is a reasonably healthy person, it may be better for the mother to release her responsiblity and allow him to live with his dad. This sharing of responsibility for parenting can provide the boy with stronger discipline. The problem, of course, is the mother's acceptance of this kind of arrangement and her overcoming of any guilt feelings about abandoning her son."

A child who has survived the upheaval of divorce may need a bit more tolerance and love as he sorts out his feelings and accepts the changes in his life style. Depending upon the child's age, love and security can be provided in a variety of ways, according to Dr. Dobbins. A pre-verbal infant is shown love through stroking; a preschooler is shown affection through his parents' participating in his games and activities; an elementary child is shown love through his parents' attending school events; an adolescent knows he is cared for when he is given a sense of privacy and trust. Although tolerance may be extended during the first few months after divorce, discipline should not be forfeited.

"The three *F's* of good discipline are: Be *fair, firm,* and *friendly.* Fairness is determined by Christian compassion—putting oneself in the child's place and saying, 'If I were two years old and living through these circumstances, what would be fair to expect of me?' Firmness can follow fair play, but should be expressed in a friendly, loving way."

Many parents don't know the difference between discipline and punishment, believes Dr. Dobbins. Discipline involves enforcement of desirable behavior by praise, commendation, or some kind of reward system. Punishment is the elimination of undesirable behavior by the infliction of emotional or physical pain. Dobbins claims just because a child is punished one may not assume he is disciplined.

"To have disciplined children, one must be a disciplined parent—one who disciplines by instruction, intervention, and example," he stresses.

Perhaps most importantly, the single mother or father should realize he or she doesn't have to be a perfect parent. By making impossible demands of herself, a mother either neglects her own life or becomes burned out in her martyr's role. Supermom often is destined for a crash landing.

"Instead of trying for perfection, try to be a 'good-enough' parent. When parents invest more in parenthood than just being good enough, they invest in diminishing returns. Such persons shortchange themselves in the development of other relationships—with God, themselves, and others. A 'good-enough' parent knows how to love and how to discipline his children."

Setting an example of discipline is not always easy for the divorced parent, suddenly deprived of both helpmate and sexual partner. Not only is the single mom or dad expected to keep the home running smoothly, the bills paid, and the children happy, but he or she is supposed to do so without the comfort and nurturing love of a spouse. The temptation to become physically involved with a new partner may be understandable, but Dr. Dobbins warns that such an involvement could be a negative influence on the children and will hurt the emotionally vulnerable single.

"The more intimate the relationship, the greater the risk of bonding two people, and the greater the risk of being hurt if the bond is broken. Bonding is like adhesive tape—the more it's used, the less it sticks. If we sow of the flesh, we reap of the flesh. If we sow of the spirit, we reap of the spirit. A physical relationship outside the realm of marriage is a risk. I tell my clients that the fewer risks they assume, the less likely they are to be hurt."

But many singles find it difficult, even impossible, to ignore their sexual needs. Some are overwhelmed by guilt and doubt that God will forgive their repeated transgressions. Whenever such fears surface during counseling sessions, Dr. Dobbins assures them of God's mercy.

"God will forgive sexual misbehavior as freely as He will a verbal mistake, but the social consequences are far more extensive. God will not remove the consequences through His forgiveness. We don't have to live with the guilt of what we've done, but we do have to live with the *results* of what we've done. As an example: If I were a drunken driver and had an accident in which I lost my eyesight, God would forgive my drunkenness, but He wouldn't restore my eyesight. Another example: After an incident of promiscuity, God would forgive the sexual misconduct, but the pregnancy that could result would remain the problem of the two sexual partners. We need to be prepared to deal with the consequences of our behavior, and if we're not prepared to do that, we ought to change our behavior. God doesn't reserve intercourse for marriage because He's mean. He does it because He's merciful. He doesn't want His children to suffer pain from what He planned for their marital pleasure."

Disciplining one's life not only reduces risks but increases self-esteem. Many singles suffer in the area of self-worth. While they may score well by the usual yardsticks of success—money, prestige, power—they feel less than successful if they've failed to establish and maintain a happy marriage. Dr. Dobbins believes that for too long, society, with the help of the media, has equated success with having a spouse, two children, a suburban split-level, and a color TV set.

"I think every person has to define success for himself or herself," he says. "We shouldn't let society dictate to us. Paul says when people 'measure themselves by themselves and compare themselves with themselves, they are without understanding' (2 Cor. 10:12 NIV). This breeds a sense of personal failure and frustration. I would encourage singles to be less ambitious in their definition of success—be more personal in it, more biblical, more realistic about it. By doing this, they'll begin seeing themselves in a more positive light. The Bible says that success can be found in a much simpler life style. 'Godliness with contentment is great gain'" (1 Tim. 6:6 NIV).

Happiness is . . . "First, a healthy relationship with God and with self," according to Dr. Dobbins. And next? "The simple things—a special friendship, the satisfaction of guiding well-adjusted children, a feeling of self-worth, a smile, a song . . . even a forty-inch muskie."

"Before singles can attract the love of others, they must see themselves as lovable. We can't do anything to make Him love us more, and we can't do anything to make Him love us less. When we accept this fact, we begin to understand God's love for us as something apart from His pleasure or displeasure with our behavior. We are lovable in God's eyes not because of what we do but because of who we are. Knowing this, we can set aside any excess from the past and get on with the business of living."

A Note of Explanation

Beginning with the May/June 1979 issue, *Solo* has featured an interview as a regular part of the magazine's format.

Although republishing them in book form was not our original idea, wide interest in the interviews and in their subject matter encouraged *Solo* and Impact Books to compile ten of the interviews into this book.

It was agreed that if the interviews were transposed from the question-answer to a third-person format, they would make for easier reading by the general public.

Holly Miller, a writer for *Saturday Evening Post,* graciously accepted the huge assignment to assist in rewriting each interview—with permission from the persons interviewed—in third-person form. Much credit for this book must go to her.

Solo is the Christian magazine for today's single adults. It is a publication of Solo Ministries, Inc., a nonprofit ministry, located at 8740 East 11th Street, Suite Q, Tulsa, Oklahoma 74112.

Further information on *Solo* magazine may be obtained from the above address.